YORK
A CITY REVEALED

LEONARD MARKHAM

SUTTON PUBLISHING

First published in 2006 by
Sutton Publishing Limited · Phoenix Mill
Thrupp · Stroud · Gloucestershire · GL5 2BU

British Library Cataloguing in Publication Data
A catalogue record for this book is available from the British Library

ISBN 0-7509-4417-X

Dedicated to my wife Lore

(and the RAF bomb-aimers who missed 85 Königstrasse)

Typeset in 11/12pt Ehrhardt.
Typesetting and origination by
Sutton Publishing Limited.
Printed and bound in England by
J.H. Haynes & Co. Ltd, Sparkford.

CONTENTS

The ancient, long-vanished doorway to Lady Irvin's mansion in Minster Yard, York.
(Drawn by H. Cave, 1811)

PREFACE

Eboracum – Eoforwic – Jorvik; so good they named it thrice, the evolving name encapsulating the growth of a 2,000-year-old city that has left its mark on England and the world. From its beginnings as a Roman legionary fortress, the city became a royal Anglo-Saxon centre, developing as a Viking trading emporium and one of the foremost cathedral cities in Europe. Strategically placed in the middle of the kingdom, it has witnessed the comings and goings of empires and myriad plots and uprisings in between. Once the seat of government, it rivalled London as England's principal city, giving its newfound name of York to the largest and arguably the most influential shire in the land.

Historically, York has more layers than a dozen pharaonic mummies, the constant unearthing of archaeological surprises adding to an international reputation crowned by a church that rivals Rome's St Peter's itself. But, there have been enough books written about York Minster alone to fill up its nave twice over, the multi-faceted output of academia ensuring that the history of the city in general is thoroughly researched and documented.

In writing this book as a non-academic, I do not aspire to compete with the many authors who have contributed so much to the knowledge and enjoyment of the great city of York. My perspective is that of an awed Yorkshireman who, as a frequent visitor, has come to know and love his capital city.

Over fifty years ago, I came first in short pants as a train spotter on the smoke-wreathed York station. I came thereafter as a lad inspired by tales of archers on the ramparts and the stand-and-deliver story of Dick Turpin on the turnpike, York's beguiling pattern of ancient streets and buildings leading me on to discover a vibrant city that somehow manages to successfully combine antiquity with modernity.

I remember York as a city that stimulated the senses, the smell of smoke and steam billowing from the 'Flying Scotsman' as she puffed off for Edinburgh combining with the sweet perfume from the nearby chocolate factories and the slightly musky odour of the turgid Ouse, to create a nasal identity that was unmistakable even with your eyes shut. And then you left the station wide-eyed to be greeted by a sight that made the heart swell, tides of daffodils, the yellow surf breaking at the foot of walls straight out of boyhood romances such as *Ivanhoe* and the *Black Arrow*, lining the way to the magnificent Minster, wherein, at Easter, the choral voices raised the roof.

York is indeed a sensual city that delights the eye with its archaeological and architectural splendour, but it is much more than that. It is a city in which the ghosts of great men haunt every street and yard. The history books of England are filled with their spirits – the Roman Emperor Constantine who took the purple here in AD 306, St Paulinus whose little wooden church blossomed into the Minster we know today, William the Conqueror who raised the still imposing Clifford's Tower, King Edward IV who was crowned in York after his victory at Hexham and, in more recent times, George Hudson, the 'Railway King', whose vision ensured that York would become a hub of the railway network.

'If you want the past,' muttered a grumpy old J.B. Priestley when he visited York in 1933, 'here it is, weighing tons.' He went on to admit in his book *English Journey* that the city had never enchanted him; many subsequent visitors who have trudged the tourist trail between dusty towers and fragmentary walls agree with the author.

A visit to this city in aspic can, I admit, be a little overpowering, dates and dynasties crowding in to obscure its interest and vitality. So, like Priestley, I'll not linger in the shadows, concentrating for the purposes of this book on the exciting

Sketch showing a dedication stone discovered under the site of a Roman temple at Toft Green, York, in 1770. The translation reads: 'This temple, sacred to the god Serapis was erected by Claudius Heronymianus lieutenant of the sixth conquering legion.' *(From* The Stranger's Guide through York and Its Cathedral 1846 – *Bellerby and Sampson's New Circulating Library, Stonegate)*

An early twentieth-century sketch showing Bootham Bar and York Minster. *(From* The Enchanting North *by J.S. Fletcher, 1908)*

modern York of the eighteenth, nineteenth and twentieth centuries, examining some of its institutions, industries, celebrities, tragedies and entertainments with stories of crimes and frivolities thrown in for good measure.

The following anonymous verse appeared in an edition of the *Saturday Review* in 1915.

> York was a capital city,
> When you were a nameless stew,
> And therefore the heart has pity,
> Dear London town for you.
> You may have Piccadilly,
> And flaunt Trafalgar Square,
> But the lily of York was a lily,
> When you were a tinkers fair!

My sentiments exactly, although I would substitute a white rose for a lily. A rose is quite as beautiful as a lily . . . but it's more masculine . . . and, in true Yorkshire tradition, has thorns.

Leonard Markham, 2006

ACKNOWLEDGEMENTS

In garnering material for this book, I have consulted widely and read copiously, my inquisitive nose and my abiding and unfailing passion and fascination for all things Tyke presenting me with a plethora of information. Every enquiry has been received with typical Yorkshire helpfulness and I would especially like to thank staff at York Central Library for their guidance, Sue Rigby of the Local Studies Centre providing a number of excellent photographs to embellish my text. I must also acknowledge the assistance received from Anne Wood who supplied similar material from the records of the *York and County Press*, and from Peter Young who made available rare illustrations from the York Minster Dean and Chapter Library. The Archiv de Hansestadt Lübeck in Germany offered me a similar service in connection with my chapter on the Baedeker Raid. In addition, I'm grateful to Betty's who supplied photographs for my chapter on their inimitable York café, and to my lifelong best friend Bernard Thompson who rescued the old drawings on pages iv, vi and 6 from oblivion.

On a personal note, I'd like to record my appreciation of the cordial welcome my wife and I received from David Hope, who entertained us in Bishopthorpe Palace before his resignation as Archbishop of York, and from Avril Pedley who escorted us on a tour of St Peter's School.

Heartfelt gratitude must go to my German wife Lore who rescued this project when it flagged, her family history providing a very personal and balanced perspective on the deadly and conflagrational wartime events of March and April 1942.

Finally, I thank the Muses for my Yorkshire lineage and heritage, hoping that they continue to lead me in many fruitful directions.

Leonard Markham

1

WHAT'S YOUR POISON?

It is an indisputable fact that in every age and in every culture the concoction of alcoholic beverages has been almost as compelling as hunger. Thousands of miles apart, separated by aeons and epochs, communities have fermented, distilled and brewed, using a variety of ingredients to create beverages that are as distinctive as civilisations themselves. But knowledge spreads as fast as conquering chiefs and legions, techniques perfected by the ancient Egyptians, Greeks and Romans percolating these shores soon after Julius Caesar's Kent invasion of 55 BC. Fortified by wine, the Roman soldiers were opposed by the Celtic hordes that were, no doubt, raised to their own furies by mead. A few decades later, after the conquest was completed, the eagle standards gave way to more disarming imagery, the signs of the vine-leafed Bacchus, the god of wine, appearing on the taverns of the newly established garrison town of Eboracum and elsewhere.

Augustinus, a retired soldier from the VI Legion based in York, would have set the pattern for generations of husbands by grabbing his dog-lead, saying goodbye to his wife Flavia Augustina and heading off to the nearest tavern. There, he would have drunk choice wines from across the empire, including vintages from Gaul, the Rhine Valley and the Jura. Transported to York in amphorae, these wines were highly resined, one recipe favouring the addition of liquid resin mixed with vine ash before fermentation. Today, a former soldier in the King's Own Yorkshire Light Infantry would drink a pint of John Smith's Bitter instead, trenching on gravy-filled Yorkshire puddings in between draughts. His imperial counterpart, though, might have enjoyed more exotic fare. Archaeological discoveries in York suggest that even in this far-flung outpost of the empire, dormice were a part of the legionary diet. These were secured alive in earthenware jars and fattened up on nuts until they were ready to eat. Also on the menu were snails and roast pigeon. Snails were fed on milk until they were too plump to retreat into their shells. Pigeons had their wings clipped or their legs broken and were reared on chewed bread. Another popular Roman delicacy was rabbit foetuses.

After the Roman legions abandoned Britain in about AD 400 the country entered the intellectually and classically devoid period of its history known as the

Dark Ages. And Eboracum, the city that had witnessed the empurpling of Emperor Constantius in AD 306 and was universally renowned as a cosmopolitan centre for trade, was looted and ravaged, the new rulers of England preferring to build their noble halls of timber rather than of stone.

Turfed out of his tavern, Bacchus was left to wander loofah-tongued for decades amid the cultural ruins. Forsaken by the far from sophisticated Anglo-Saxons, who preferred ale to wine, he had to cultivate a new palate, but by the time of the arrival of the Vikings in York in the mid-ninth century he was beginning to appreciate the native brew. The Norsemen imported some Rhenish wine in barrels and amphorae into York but they too drank copious quantities of ale, one aristocrat of their number, an Anglo-Danish Earl named Ulfp or Ulf, leaving us a large inscribed and decorated drinking horn that survives in the Minster's undercroft to this day.

Later, the monks of the newly Christianised nation created their monasteries and the first purpose-built brew-houses, offering hospitality to visitors and travellers alike. No self-respecting abbot would produce an unpalatable pint. Indeed, his head brewer had to swear four times to God on the purity of his ale, and to mark his barrels with four crosses. Some of the brewers, though, in religious establishments such as the Benedictine monastery of St Mary's in York, were tainted with rather dubious reputations. Founded in about 1085, St Mary's had become a centre for heavy drinking and licentiousness, Thurstan, the Archbishop of York, carrying out an inspection and complaining: 'The whole Chapter House rang with such a tumult and confusion that it seemed more like the seditious uproar of drunken revellers than the humility of monks.' But Bacchus was a convert and 'upon the hogshead he got astride and proclaimed the ale was deified'.

By this time, York had a number of monastic establishments and the city had grown prosperous as a centre for the wool trade. The generated wealth funded the building of the Minster and financed the Merchant Adventurers' business enterprises in the Mediterranean, the Middle East and Russia. York blossomed as a marketplace for all manner of goods, and the number of taverns, their proprietors adapting the brewing techniques developed by the monks, increased dramatically to cater for the influx of traders. With an eye to quick profits, some unscrupulous publicans watered down their ale but the practice was outlawed in the thirteenth century. An annual Assize of Ale introduced by Henry III charged the Sheriff of York with tasting each brew for strength! Diluted, adulterated and just plain bad, beer was always a problem in a city that drew its water from the polluted waters of the Ouse, one later remedy suggesting the following: 'To twelve or fourteen gallons of beer add (by pouring in at the bung hole) a large spoonful of flour of mustard . . . stop it well up; and in twenty-four hours the beer will be thin and clear without any unpleasant taste.'

But assizes did not just deal with the relatively trivial problems of beer. The more sober variety, the regional sessions of the judges of the superior courts, were first introduced as a consequence of Magna Carta in 1215. They regularly visited York and from 1379 condemned felons convicted of the worst crimes to be executed on the Knavesmire. A large, open tract of pastureland located south of the city, the Knavesmire regularly witnessed the awful jamboree that attended disembowellings and hangings. York publicans have never been known to look gift-horses in the mouth, and those whose taverns were on the route to Tyburn or in the vicinity of the vile places where corpses were hung for weeks made fortunes by selling ale to the crowds. By way of entertainment in some inns, executions were re-enacted, and ballad-mongers peddled excruciating verses allegedly quoting the dying words of victims. Side by side with horse racing, which began on the Knavesmire in 1731, the executions continued until 1801.

The next big commercial opportunity for York innkeepers came at the close of the Civil War. Soon after King Charles lost his head in 1649, a stagecoach service was established for the first time on some of the major roads leading out of London, the 200-mile, four-day journey between the capital and York on the Great North Road becoming one of the most famous in the country. State-of-the-art travel had arrived, links were established with Hull and Doncaster and York inns such as the Black Swan in Coney Street and the Punch Bowl in Blossom Street were quickly established to cater for the increasingly discerning demands of travellers. In 1706, there were probably not more than half a dozen coaches operating in the whole of Yorkshire, but even by that date, the Black Swan had established a reputation for hospitality. In 1754, coaches were fitted with springs and road surfaces were improved by the pioneering engineer McAdam, four principal inns catering for the trade in York. Stage and light coaches were the speciality of the Black Swan. The York Tavern dealt with mail traffic. The posting business was attended to by the George, and Etteridge's provided relays of horses for the nobility and gentry travelling in private carriages. Over a few decades, the inn became as much a part of the English character as roast beef and

Yorkshire pudding, and some inns were celebrated in works of fiction. When Charles Dickens's *Pickwick Papers* first appeared in 1837, they were still enjoying their heyday. Dickens came to York towards the end of the coaching era in 1838, just three years before the opening of the North Midland Railway. He probably travelled by the 'Wellington', coming to Yorkshire to gather information for his new book about the brutalities of life in private schools. Having dined in the Ancient Unicorn in Bowes and having met his inspiration for Squeers in the nearby academy, he returned to the Black Swan in York and began cogitating on ideas for *Nicholas Nickleby*. The Black Swan was described as a 'place of good entertainment for man or

The author Charles Dickens 'baited' at the *Black Swan*. (*From* With Dickens in Yorkshire *by T.P. Cooper, 1923*)

beast'. A commodious place, it provided stabling for over 100 horses, let alone the other notable men who also enjoyed its charms. Thomas Carlyle came here in 1820, and during the 1840s the ebullient James Boyle, fifth Earl of Glasgow was a frequent visitor during race weeks. An irritable and irascible man who was used to getting his own way, the Earl once famously threw an incompetent waiter through a ground-floor window. The innkeeper gingerly complained about Glasgow's action but, unrepentant, he rejoined with the words: 'All right, what's the cost?' 'Let's say £5', answered the innkeeper. 'Well, put it on the bill!' volleyed Glasgow. His host did just that, entering a charge under the sundries heading: 'Breaking waiter's arm – £5.' In 1852, the rather unfortunate Poet Laureate Alfred Lord Tennyson took a room at the Black Swan during an election contest, describing afterwards how he had to plunge through a brawling melee of voters to get to his dinner. The 'glazed hats of policemen, like sunshine here and there at the breaking up of a storm', allowed him to get to his trencher in one piece.

The coaching era produced many wonderful characters. Post-boys were responsible for riding postilion, for assisting passengers, paying toll fees and returning horses to their own stables. Coach drivers, the so-called 'knights of the road', had the difficult job of managing the teams of horses and ensuring speed and passenger safety. The most famous of their number in York was Tom Holtby.

This crack driver had a reputation as a showman, his bravado and finesse on the reins earning him the nickname of 'Rash Tom'. By the age of 30 he was recognised as the best coachman around. He had a long association with the 'Edinburgh Mail' and could cover the 197 miles between London and York in a respectable twenty hours fifty-four minutes. The 'Edinburgh Mail' rattled on between 1786 and its last outing in 1842, when Holtby ceremoniously pulled into the yard of the Black Swan with a black flag flying.

York's most celebrated hostelry sold vast quantities of ale, and its sales received a further boost when the social evils of drinking gin – the so-called 'mother's ruin' – were recognised by Parliament. Such was the polluted state of the town's water that gin was the preferred tipple of much of the local population, including children. Landowners actively encouraged gin production as it consumed vast quantities of corn. In addition the spirit was so ridiculously cheap – it was hardly worth smuggling – that at the height of the gin era between 1740 and 1742, it has been estimated that, in some inner-city areas, it accounted for twice as many deaths as births. The government decided to do something and an Act of Parliament in 1751 greatly increased the tax on spirits. The Beerhouse Act of 1830 further reduced the demand in favour of the amber nectar by halving the duty on beer and actively encouraging any person of good character to apply for a beer-house licence costing 2 guineas. Within twelve weeks of the act becoming law, 25,000 licences had been granted in England and Wales, and the walking distance between the taverns on Walmgate – that street alone had twenty-six licensed premises in 1800! – and Pavement became even shorter. With the opening of the railway in 1839, the need for larger commercial hotels sparked a new wave of development, further enhancing the rich mix of licensed premises that endures to this day.

A number of personal accounts by York publicans and their families during the war years shed light on a profession that has always demanded hard work and dedication. One illuminating story that caught my eye was told by a lady whose family ran the Lion and Lamb on Blossom Street. On the day her husband died in October 1914, fifty soldiers and their horses were compulsorily billeted at the inn, the young widow having to cater for their every need. And there was beer rationing! During the next conflict the army was still there, diaries of the time recording the comings and goings of military men and vehicles, some carrying the top-secret remains of shot-down Luftwaffe aircraft. I must refer to one other interesting snippet from 1939. In that awesome year, the Brown Cow pub on Hope Street installed six dartboards for a contest that was broadcast live on radio!

So, now let me take you on a short tour of some of York's intoxicating past. The city has more than its fair share of churches and museums, but if you like to take your history with a splash of something more stimulating than holy water, try a cocktail of its inns instead. If the cherubic Mr Pickwick loved the English inn, and he did, right down to his popping waistcoat buttons, he would have adored the inns of York, for York still has more atmospheric inns than any other city in the country. Pity then that what would have been the jewel in the licensed crown was demolished in 1868. The George Inn on Coney Street was one of the most colourful and exuberant buildings in the city, having crests above its entrance doors and gables and bargeboards smothered in richly decorated carvings. Thankfully, though, many other precious premises have survived.

One historic inn has the dubious distinction of being the most flooded in England, the frequent inundations of the Ouse which flows within a few feet of the King's Arms being recorded on a board in its bar. For three centuries, the river has spilled into its cellars, the inn overlooking the point on King's Staith where King Richard III reputedly disembarked on his journeys to his boyhood home in Middleham Castle, near Leyburn. Beer barrels are kept dry in one of its upstairs rooms that once doubled as a morgue for criminals executed on the nearby bridge.

Try the seventeenth-century Punch Bowl in Stonegate next. It was built alongside the route used to take stone from the river for the construction of the Minster. A quaint and interesting old inn with many period features, it was once the popular haunt of the Minster's bell ringers. At the time renovations were under way in 1765, the ringers donated a redundant tenor bell clapper from the Minster, the clapper now helping to support one of the building's main beams.

On to the grimly named Hole-in-the-Wall on High Petergate. It resounds to darker echoes from York's past. Within a hundred or so yards of the Minster, its name recalls the time when part of the building was used as a prison for fallen clergy who received their meals through the eponymous hole in the wall. The pub was connected with the Minster by secret tunnels, long since sealed.

Raise a fourth pint in the Little John in Castlegate. It was established in about 1730 as a coaching inn, a pick-up point for the 'Providence' taking passengers to link with the Hull Packet, and for the 'Antelope' connecting with Leeds. Paradoxically, until the late nineteenth century, it was called the Robin Hood, its new sign chirpily reading: 'Robin Hood is dead and gone, now come and drink with Little John'. Customers here would have toasted one of the city's historic

The long demolished George Inn on Coney Street, York. *(Drawn by H. Cave, 1811)*

moments when the hanged body of John Palmer, alias Dick Turpin, was brought to the nearby Blue Boar on 10 April 1739.

Step out and round the corner into the quaint bar of the seventeenth-century Three Tuns in Coppergate – mind the sloping floor now! – and raise a glass to Eric the Headcleaver whose ancestors' Viking bones lie deep beneath your feet.

Then wobble on to Young's Hotel in Petergate. Another nefarious character linked with a York inn was born here in 1570, Guy Fawkes going on to be educated as St Peter's School before his escapade in the Houses of Parliament.

The Roman Bath in Sampson's Square, York, has a legionary bathhouse in its cellar.
(Leonard Markham Archive (LMA))

Finally, down your seventh jar in the Roman Bath in Sampson's Square. It has had various names since it was first erected in about 1783. It was refurbished in 1930, astonished workers discovering part of a Roman bath 15 feet below street level. Now on display, the bath probably belonged to a private residence and was not part of the military garrison, although tiles were found close by, imprinted with the mark of the IX Legion. Further archaeological finds suggest that the later VI Legion also helped with construction.

If you need a nightcap and sometimes only a couple of whisky chasers will do, you will find plenty of spirits in the Old White Swan in Goodramgate and the York Arms in High Petergate, remembering that there are more haunted licensed premises in York that you can shake a bulb of garlic at. The former is regularly attended by a multitude of ghosts in period dress and, after closing time, its stools are often arranged in semi-circles. Sometimes, its attic windows smash simultaneously. Meanwhile, the disruptive Grey Lady stalks the corridors of the York Arms, throwing objects around and turning off the gas taps.

If such spirits leave you cold and you want to eschew tradition and enjoy an ambience more stainless steel minimalist than carved mahogany, enter the glitzy portals of Kennedy's Wine Bar off Stonegate or Ziggy's on Micklegate, going on to experience the delights of the wonderfully named young persons' pub crawl known as the Micklegate Run. John Smith's Bitter from Tadcaster, Cracker, York Bitter, Black Bess Stout, Centurion's Ghost or Wonkey Donkey – all from York's own brewery opened in 1996 – or Semillon Chardonnay – what's *your* poison?

2
SEE SWELLS

Yawn . . . yawn . . . a chapter on the office of Archbishop of York. How boring. But no! Wake up at the back, for there is nothing here that would induce sleep. Far from being the boring old spare parts of history, the archbishops have led stirring and adventurous lives every bit as exciting as the heroes of fiction.

Ninety-six archbishops have been entrusted with the holy crosier since Paulinus first took office in the year 625. His was a remarkable act to follow. He brought Christianity to the north of England, converted King Edwin and led him from his palace at Londesborough to the ruins of the old legionary fortress in York. Here, they erected a tiny wooden church that would eventually blossom into the Minster. Paulinus became a saint and established a bishopric that has been known ever since as the 'Chair of Paulinus'. Remarkably, four out of five of his immediate successors – Archbishops Chad, Wilfred I, John of Beverley and Wilfred II – were also canonised.

Some rare-named priests were installed in subsequent years – Ethelbald, Osketyl, Ealdwulf, Aelfric Puttoc and Cynesige – their far-flung diocese embracing both York and Hexham. The spiritual and temporal roles of the office were gradually developed, the archbishops of York and Canterbury vying for the moral and political ascendancy. Archbishops became superintendents of religious affairs in their dioceses but they also became politically powerful and influential, taking their seats in the ancient great councils that advised the monarch and subsequently joining the elite of the aristocracy in the House of Lords.

The post of Archbishop of York became one of the most coveted in the land, the attendant kudos and luxurious lifestyle attracting men of great intellect, breeding, accomplishments and profound ambition. The archbishopric was a rich and vast one, encompassing over two million acres of land and hundreds of clergy and churches, and in 1216 when Walter De Grey was enthroned, he was able to purchase land to enrich his position even further. A few miles downstream from York, he bought the manor of Thorpe St Andrew from the monks of Kirkstall Abbey near Leeds. He gave it the new name of Bishopthorpe and ordered the erection of a grand palace to augment the accommodation next to the Minster. Bishopthorpe Palace has been their graces' main home ever since, their property in central York lingering on until the 1560s when it was finally abandoned. The palace was briefly in private ownership after it was sold for £567 to the Roundhead Colonel Walter White in 1647. He extended the building on the south

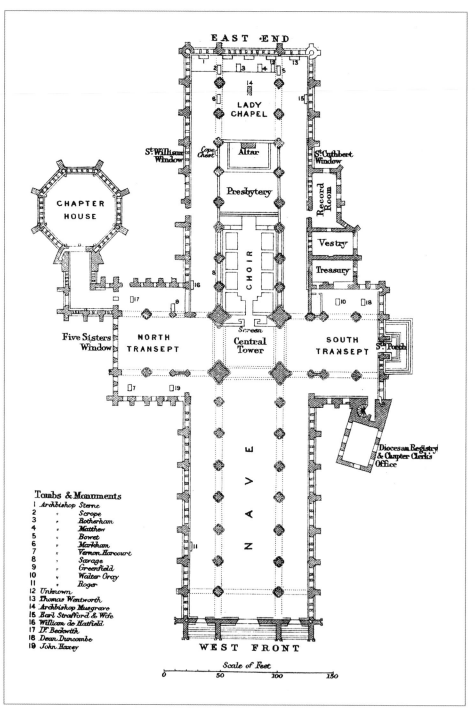

This nineteenth-century plan of York Minster shows the locations of twelve archbishops' tombs. (*From the* Through Guide Series – *Yorkshire Part I by J.B. Baddeley, 1893*)

side of the north range by adding two wings but by the time it reverted to ecclesiastical use at the Restoration, it was in a poor state of repair.

When viewed from a modern perspective, there appears to be a jarring contradiction between the hedonism and religious hegemony that were integral facets of the role of the archbishop in those early days and the purely spiritual motivation that inspires the office today. This notion is further strengthened in realising that the archbishops had, in addition to the palace at Bishopthorpe, other opulent residences elsewhere.

Close to Bishopthorpe, the archbishops built a comfortable retreat at Cawood. East of York, they developed Yorkshire's first holiday complex at a place newly named Bishop Wilton at a time when the 'holy-day' thoughts of ordinary people extended only to prayer, penance and cold fish. Such was their wealth and opportunity for ecclesiastical delegation that they could afford to decamp to the country for part of the summer months to enjoy quiet reflection and a little hunting in the nearby deer park. They also had palaces in Ripon and Otley and a sumptuous residence – York Place – in London. All these properties had lavish kitchens and wine cellars, the palace in Otley for a time outdoing the rest.

A view from the Garrowby Hill summit over the village of Bishop Wilton and the Plain of York. The Archbishops of York had a summer palace here on a preserved site between the village and the buildings in the foreground. York Minster can be seen to the south-west on a clear day. *(LMA)*

Archbishop Henry Bowett – unflatteringly known to history as the 'Bibacious Prelate' – made extensive additions to the kitchens and cellars in his Otley palace to accommodate his enormous appetite for fine food and strong drink. Claret was his favourite tipple and he is estimated to have consumed annually some fourscore tuns of the stuff – and each barrel or tun contained some 252 gallons – together with a goodly amount of port. But that was as a spit in the ocean compared with the mitred slurping that took place during the mother of all blowouts held at Cawood to mark the installation of Archbishop George Neville, the brother of the Earl of Warwick. In procuring food for the banquet, half the entire food stocks in the county were raided, 62 cooks, 515 kitchen hands and 1,000 waiters producing one of the biggest feasts in history. The first course gobbled up a whole forest in fuel, 1,000 sides of mutton, 6 wild bulls, 304 joints of pork, 204 kids and 12 porpoises and seals. The second course disposed of 400 swans, 2000 geese, 4,000 rabbits, 1,000 capons, 1000 egrets, 104 peacocks, 400 heron, myriads of other birds and 5,500 venison pasties. To finish off, the guests were served 5,000 custards, 4,000 baked tarts and spices and sugared delicacies and wafers galore. All this was washed down with 300 tuns of ale, 100 tuns of wine and a pipe (105 gallons) of hippocras, a 'one-for-the-road' cordial drink made with wine flavoured with spices. Add all this up and you get a staggering 100,905 gallons of booze. Some party! Some hangover!

Like their feasting, the archbishops were larger than life and some of them were pompous and arrogant in the extreme. Ealdred, who was consecrated in 1061, took umbrage when a delivery of his provisions was waylaid by the King's men and diverted to the royal granaries in York Castle. The Archbishop was outraged and complained to the local sheriff – to no avail. Undaunted, he set off for London with a train of ecclesiastics and barged his way into the royal chambers with little ceremony, threatening to curse the King. The terrified monarch fell prostrate and repenting, much to the amazement of the outraged nobility, for this was the same William who had conquered England. Vastly resenting the prelate's arrogance, they urged the King to get to his feet, Ealdred intervening with the admonishment: 'Let him alone! Let him lie! He has not fallen at my feet but at the feet of St Peter.' Soon afterwards, the Archbishop's goods were restored.

In researching the holy lineage, one cannot help but gain the impression that sometimes the office see-sawed between debauchery and divinity, saints and sinners occupying the archbishop's throne almost in successive appointments. In 1143, William FitzHerbert, the Treasurer of York Minster and King Stephen's Chaplain, was consecrated as Archbishop of York. The local monks, represented by the Archdeacon of York, Osbert de Baines, complained to the Pope about regal favouritism and William was deposed to a life of prayer and religious study in Winchester. Recalled to the see in 1154, he died in suspicious circumstances just a few months later, accusers alleging that he drank from a chalice poisoned by Osbert. The charges were never proved, but Osbert's reputation was blighted and he was unfrocked. In the next few years, the character of William was thoroughly rehabilitated and eventually he was canonised as St William of York. Numerous miracles are attributed to this holy man. A divine intercession on Ouse Bridge is perhaps the best remembered. On his return from his ordination by the Pope in Rome, William was besieged by a large crowd gathered on the rickety wooden structure that spanned the river. Such was the tumult of the reception that the bridge collapsed, spilling men, women, children and horses into the rolling flood in 'one tangled, shrieking mass'. Unperturbed, St William raised his crucifix aloft and intoned a prayer, all the people escaping from the river as if they were walking on dry land. The only casualty was a single horse, which broke its leg.

Alexander Neville, who took office in 1374, was a more cantankerous and irritable priest than most. No sooner had he been appointed than he quarrelled with his entire staff and retinue. He fell out with the Dean and Chapter of the Minster, denounced the Treasurer, criticised the canons of Beverley and Ripon, and slated the citizens of York. But his most vehement condemnation, deserving of hell fire and damnation, was reserved for the merchants of Hull. Their crime? They dared to dispense with the ancient custom of *prisage*, whereby the archbishop could claim two free casks of wine from every ship of 20 tons' burden or more landing its cargo at the port. The canny captains of Hull circumvented the custom by unloading their casks in the estuary and bringing them ashore in small boats. Neville was outraged and set off for Hull mob-handed and in high dudgeon to meet the Mayor of Hull, Sir Thomas de Waltham. 'When flint strikes flint', records one report, 'sparks fly.' Neville immediately began berating the mayor and seemed to be getting the better of the verbal exchange until one of his entourage grinned in victory, causing an incensed Sir Thomas to grab the crosier and go on the rampage, the Archbishop tossing off his cope and joining in the brawl. Sir Thomas and his men, however, got the better of their opponents, one unlucky clergyman having the crosier broken across his shoulders. Retreating under a barrage of blows, Neville called off his protest and returned to York. But he was not done yet. He quickly complained to the King and the Mayor of Hull was summoned to Westminster to explain his actions before a legal tribunal, the court deciding that the case was to be 'left in abeyance'. Neville had to forgo his wine, but on his return to Hull the Mayor was given a rapturous reception by the merchants who broached a cask of wine in celebration – and they all grinned.

Richard Scrope, who took office in 1398, was heavily involved in a plot to oust King Henry IV. He posted notices on the doors of the churches in York and elsewhere charging the King with usurpation, murder, perjury and extortion, and took part in a bloodless insurrection against the royal forces in 1405. Duped by the King's army with promises that all grievances would be remedied, he and his allies laid down their arms. They were promptly arrested. Scrope was ignominiously taken back to Bishopthorpe Palace and tried in its dining room in the presence of the King. Found guilty of treason, he was summarily taken from the place and beheaded in a field close to York. This was the first time that a prelate had suffered capital punishment in England. There is a sad and macabre poem affixed to the wall of the Great Hall of Bishopthorpe Palace. It refers to 'five strokys' of the axe, Scrope having requested the executioner, in allusion to the Five Wounds of Christ, to cut off his head with five strokes. The inhabitants of the city were also chastised when its traders were deprived of their royal franchises.

At times, the responsibilities of the Archbishop of York were crushingly onerous, the need for ecclesiastical and political attentiveness and acuity demanding sobriety, seriousness and solemnity. The office inspired dolefulness in some incumbents but in others it merely served to heighten their penchant for mirth. Tobias Matthew, who was archbishop from 1606, was, at times, an ardent and sobersides preacher whose legendary sermons were delivered from nearly every 'pulpit in the wide dioceses of Durham and York'. But he was also an inveterate punster who passed on his rather jauntily worn mitre in 1628.

After Matthew's office became vacant, Charles I was puzzled about who should follow. He naturally sought advice, referring the question of the succession to the distinguished Right Revd Dr Mountain, a Cawood farmer's son who had pulled himself up by his bootstraps to become, in turn, the Bishop of Lincoln, Durham and London. 'Hadst thou faith as a grain of mustard seed, Your Majesty', responded the good doctor with unabashed levity, 'thou wouldst say to this Mountain (at the same time laying his hand on his breast), be thou removed and cast into the see.' It is recorded that the King laughed heartily and duly made the

A monastic depiction of Archbishop Richard Scrope in a precious illuminated manuscript known as *The Bolton Hours*. Found guilty of treason, the archbishop had his head removed with 'five strokys' of the axe. *(Reproduced by kind permission of the Dean and Chapter of York)*

right appointment, fulfilling Mountain's prophecy: 'Lincoln was and London is and York shall be.'

With their zeal, oratory and good example, most archbishops have led the Christian crusade in the north of England, some of their good works affecting history more than a thousand sermons. Towards the end of his office in 1691, John Sharp performed an act of Solomonic compassion and understanding that continues to inspire his successors to this day.

It was his custom to ride ahead of his official carriage on a horse. He was abroad one day travelling in this manner when he was accosted by a lone rider, the man pulling out a loaded pistol with a violent demand for money. With great fortitude and composure, Archbishop Sharp politely asked the highwayman to remove the gun and explain what prompted him to steal. The thief responded by cocking his pistol and snatching the Archbishop's purse. 'Hear me,' said the venerable prelate, 'I am Sharp, the Archbishop of York, an old man and my life is of little consequence; yours seems far otherwise. Now tell me how much you want to make you independent of so dangerous and destructive a course. I will not injure you but prove a friend.'

'Oh sir', answered the man, 'I detest this business as much as you do but there are creditors who will not wait. Taking into account what is already in your purse, I need a total of £50.' The balance was duly promised and on the appointed day, the robber presented himself before the Archbishop to collect the money with the sincerest thanks. Nothing was heard of the man for a year and a half. Then one morning he arrived abruptly at the Archbishop's door and dropped to his knees in contrition, saying: 'In me my lord, you now behold what was once most wretched; now by your inexpressible humanity, rendered equal, perhaps superior to millions. Oh my lord, 'tis you, 'tis you that have saved me, body and soul.' With that he proffered £50 to his benefactor, explaining that providence had brought him a fortune, the wisdom and generosity of the Archbishop making him the most penitent, the most grateful and the happiest of human beings.

Some other remarkable characters have since occupied the archbishop's throne, the order of merit for improbability being headed by Lancelot Blackburn, whose adventures were every bit as exciting as those of the Arthurian knight. Born Lancelot Muggins, the man who would become Archbishop of York was educated at Christ Church, Oxford. He left that establishment under a cloud, and having stolen a fiddle from one of his tutors he headed off to London to seek his fortune. Singing and playing for his supper for a while, he quit the capital, securing a job as an apprentice seaman aboard the *Fair Sally*, a collier bound for London. The vessel was intercepted off Scarborough by the pirate schooner *Black Broom*, commanded by the notorious 'Redmond of the Red Hand', and that might have been the end of young Muggins but for his hidden talents. Recruited to the cut-throats' ranks, he displayed a natural talent for swashbuckling and before long he became the captain of the *Black Broom* and the scourge of every merchant in Europe, sweeping the seas from Cyprus to Cape Wrath. And he played his fiddle all the while! Retiring from the sea, he set up as a country gentleman at the foot of the Yorkshire Wolds and changed his name to Blackburn in an oblique reference to the name of his former ship. But bucolic pursuits failed to engage his restless spirit for long, and, repenting of his deeds, he began to study for the priesthood. Blackburn never did things by halves – 'he had already become notorious as a seeker of clerical plums' – and by 1724 had become Archbishop of York, much to the incredulity of his friends and victims. It is even alleged that he employed the highwayman Dick Turpin as his palace butler! To celebrate his advancement, Blackburn returned his beloved fiddle to its rightful owner in a new, exquisitely figured leather case. He also arranged that an effigy of himself, fiddle in hand, be erected in York Minster. He is known to posterity as the 'Jolly old archbishop of York' and the 'Buccaneer Bishop'. Somewhat disparagingly, he was said to have 'gained more hearts than souls', but he was a remarkable man. After his death, a poem was published in 1743 alluding to his worldly ways. It was entitled: 'Priestcraft and Lust or Lancelot to his Ladies, an Epistle from the Shades'.

In 1761, a totally different character came to Bishopthorpe. The wealthy and aristocratic Robert Hay Drummond entertained lavishly and lived the life of a lord. He visited all the gentry in Yorkshire and Nottinghamshire and stayed as a guest for long periods at Castle Howard and Temple Newsam House near Leeds. His successor William Markham was more different still: a notorious nepotist, he was pompous, arrogant, bad-tempered and indolent. He participated in the Gordon Riots, Horace Walpole consigning the prelate's reputation as a firebrand to the history books with the appellation 'that warlike metropolitan Archbishop Turpin'. Even Markham's surviving bust shows a crabby old dog!

The next incumbent, Edward Venables Vernon-Harcourt, was as terrifying as his name. At the age of 92, he was walking with his chaplain across a wooden bridge over an ornamental pond in Bishopthorpe Palace grounds when it collapsed, and both men plunged up to their necks in water. Harcourt spluttered: 'I think we've frightened the frogs.'

Down the centuries, the office of the Archbishop of York has been filled by saints, rogues, playboys and reformers who, despite disgrace and decapitation, have kept the flame of Christianity alive. It may have guttered on occasions but a succession of outstanding men with true vocation, zeal, energy, talent and real charisma has regained the holy ground.

One man who rekindled the spirit of Paulinus was William Thomson. A tireless, self-effacing pioneer, especially of educational and moral reform, he became known to the working classes as 'Our Archbishop', although his initial welcome was far from cordial. At the time he took office in 1863, the burgeoning populations of Britain's industrial cities had outrun the provision of churches and in some quarters there was widespread indifference to religion bordering on antagonism. In Hull there was just one church for every 8,500 people; in Middlesbrough there was one for every 10,000 and in Sheffield one for every 8,000. Things were so bad in the Steel City that one clergyman refused to go there unless he had some guarantee of his personal safety. But with warnings of lawlessness and rejection ringing in his ears, the undaunted Thomson visited Sheffield, the story of his encounter on the street with a mechanic and his son emphasising the measure of his task.

The mechanic passed Thomson by without even a flicker of acknowledgement. His son, though, touched his cap in deference, the indignant father clipping the boy's ear with the words: 'If I sees ya touching ya cap again to a parson, my lad, I'll give thee summat to remember a parson by.' Undeterred, Thomson began his ministry, taking on a ferocious workload. He toured and lectured widely on a wide range of subjects, giving expositions on art and science, musical progress, Sunday closing and the vices of gambling and drinking. Never hectoring, he readily engaged his congregations with sincerity, tenderness, kindliness and supreme piety, and they loved him for it. 'I'm going to talk to you in a language you and I both understand,' he announced at the start of one of his first speaking engagements before a working-class congregation in Sheffield. 'There will be no attempt at condescension.' He went on to re-energise religious teaching in those Yorkshire places where Christianity had fallen into disrepute, and he made particular friends in Sheffield where one assembly was described as being like a 'gate of stars fronting the sun that receives and renders back'. His many admirers presented him with a gift of cutlery in 1883 and when he died in 1890, sixteen working men carried his coffin to his grave in Bishopthorpe.

Another pious archbishop who brought dignity and devotion to his office was Cosmo Gordon Lang, who came to Bishopthorpe in 1909. Forsaking a profitable career as an attorney, he was an able and tireless worker who helped formulate the far-reaching Marriage Laws. Lang was an expert theologian but he had some endearing idiosyncrasies. High technology was definitely not his suit! He was once presented with a Gillette Safety Razor but he used the device only once, the intricacies of inserting a new blade proving beyond him. He had similar problems with another mechanical gift – a beautiful gold fountain pen. He used it until the ink ran out and kept it thereafter in his attaché case for twenty-seven years. The archbishop travelled thousands of dutiful miles. In the summer of 1915, at the invitation of Lord Jellicoe, he visited the Grand Fleet in Scapa Flow, Invergordon and Rosyth, enjoying a whole month with the sailors. Two years later he made the journey to the Western Front, where he gave a memorable address to six brigades of the Fifth Army before they went into action. He also went to the Somme, Messines and Vimy battlegrounds. During one of his sermons, his congregation came under fire, and a shell dropped just 50 yards from his lectern.

Jimmy Cagney in a frock – Cosmo Gordon Lang, the Bishop of Stepney who later became Archbishop of York. (From Cosmo Gordon Lang by J.G. Lockhart, 1949)

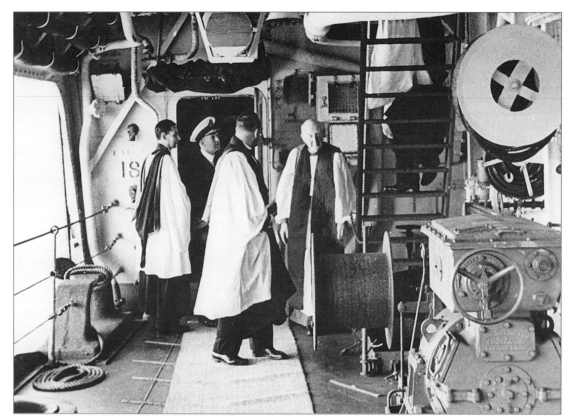

Archbishop Garbett on board the warship HMS *Venerable* in 1945. *(Reproduced by kind permission of the Dean and Chapter of York)*

Lang passed the mitre to William Temple in 1929, one of his successors, Dr John Habgood, describing Temple – 'The People's Archbishop' – as the most impressive in the long history of the office. 'He was a world figure and a large man in every sense,' said Dr Habgood. 'A good philosopher and theologian, he was a social figure too, and one of the founders of the World Council of Churches. Temple combined great abilities with a very warm temperament.'

Cyril Foster Garbett succeeded Temple in 1942. In the great Yorkshire tradition, he was a plain and brave speaker and a man of great intellect and some notoriety. Winston Churchill once described him as 'The Archiepiscopal Ulysses'. Globe-trotting Garbett – he visited Russia, the USA, Canada, Australia and the Pacific, the West Indies and the Middle East – always followed his conscience and unashamedly mixed religion with politics, often putting his own reputation on the line. He wrestled with the ethics of Britain's drive to nuclear parity and in a landmark speech in the Lords on 16 March 1955 put the case for deploying the hydrogen bomb. The speech was denounced in a torrent of letters from outraged pacifists, Roman Catholics and Jews, but Garbett's courageous and forthright views were applauded in the House and in the press. The Archbishop later wrote in his diary: 'My reason tells me that the line I took was right, namely that with the bomb there was less risk of war than without it, and that its protection gives us one more chance of peace-making: but I wish I could simply have denounced the whole thing as evil.' And, fifty years ahead of his time, Garbett's views on the conflict between Arabs and Jews were similarly passionate and balanced. He was denounced as an anti-Zionist on both sides of the Atlantic, many violent and abusive Jews resenting his pro-Arab speeches in the House of Lords. One extract from a speech delivered on 5 November 1953 has immediate resonance today:

> The civilised world has been horrified by the destruction of the small Arab village of Quibya on the borders of the state of Israel and the cruel massacre of its inhabitants, men, women and children. There seems little doubt that this was carried out by the regular forces of Israel and was not a raid by a few irresponsible terrorists. For many months past there have been acts of violence committed by both sides but this in its calculated horror is different in degree. It is well that the State of Israel should realise the disquiet and indignation caused on both sides of the Atlantic by this brutal act; and this has not been lessened by its failure to express any regret. The whole position in Palestine is profoundly unsatisfactory . . .

The tenor of the speech hit home. Just a few days later, the State of Israel was censored by the United Nations Security Council. Wherever injustice reared its head, Garbett was there in the thick of the denunciations, military atrocities in Korea and Yugoslavia also drawing his ire. *The Times* referred to the Archbishop's contributions as 'the most relevant contribution of Christianity to the discussion of world politics'.

Household names Ramsey, Coggan, Blanch and Habgood built on the reputation of Garbett and helped bring a more modern Church through the troublesome last decades of the twentieth century, the issues of dwindling congregations, religious irrelevance and secularism, women clergy, homosexuality, moral bankruptcy, political correctness, alternative spiritualities, the rise of Islam, loss of family values and the overwhelming materialism of society rocking the Church to its very foundations. In 1995, David Hope from Wakefield took on the awesome responsibility of steering his mightily assailed Church into the twenty-first century. Before his surprise resignation in 2004, I met His Grace in Bishopthorpe Palace to get a progress report.

A devout and courteous man with immense responsibility that encompassed 600 churches in Yorkshire alone, Archbishop Hope looked out over the Ouse from his first-floor study and spoke eloquently about his office, citing Lang and Temple as two of the most influential archbishops of modern times. Asked about the relevance of Christianity in a world fractured by modern problems, he responded thoughtfully suggesting that church attendance was no longer the sole measure of interest in the spiritual life. In the wider context, he suggested that the seeds of faith needed to be nurtured wherever people met and that the Church should act as a broker between factions, explaining the need for 'connectedness and continuity and a willingness to engage with people' whether they be religious leaders, politicians, businessmen, single parents or drug addicts. The important thing was, said the archbishop,

> that God works in a variety of situations; we must allow Him to flourish. And do you know something? When asked, 70 per cent of people in this country voluntarily say they are Christian. We're seeing a far more committed membership of the Church today. People are looking for meaning. Young people especially are asking about issues to do with the future of the planet. What happens when the oil runs out? They're sometimes more concerned about practical issues concerning the environment than morality but there is a bigger interest than ever in spirituality.

On the question of intolerance and enmity between opposing world faiths, the Archbishop suggested: 'Religion is like the weather. It can be very good or very bad and stormy. There is a return of religious fanaticism but it means that those of us who can must build bridges and keep the dialogue going. And I would remind everyone – Christians, Jews and Muslims – that we all originate from the one Father of Faith – Abraham. We are all called upon to be ambassadors of God.'

On the more domestic issues of family disintegration, secularism and political correctness – 'Yes! PC has gone mad!' exclaimed the Archbishop, pointing to the need for a greater awareness of personal responsibility, such initiatives as the Church-sponsored Year of the Family and the Alpha and Emmaus courses helping to give direction.

A forthright and a thoroughly affable man who, in hindsight, hinted at the stifling bureaucracy of his position – he worked an onerous seven-day week and received nearly 2,000 items of correspondence every month – Archbishop Hope spoke highly of York and his native county. 'What do I like about Yorkshire? Well, as a Wakefield lad born and bred I like its grittiness and straightforwardness. Its people are straight on the whole and there is a certain reality about things.' With that, he took me on a guided tour of the palace, showing me the centuries-old chapel and the Great Hall where Richard Scrope's trial took place. There, set into the vast riverside window, twinkling out on to the beautifully manicured lawns, is the ill-fated archbishop's crest in stained glass, the device taking its place alongside the arms of other archbishops, the richly endowed panes including one recently dedicated to Archbishop Hope. The composition reflects his heritage and interests. A pyramid of interlocking stones alludes to his father's profession as a builder and his own personal interest in hill walking. The inclusion of a fleur-de-lis device borrowed from the coat of arms of Wakefield honours his home town.

'And what of the cross keys?'

'The gold one is the key of Heaven; the silver one is the key of Hell.' Finally, I asked the Archbishop if he had a message for the people of York. He was quite prophetic in his answer. 'The office of archbishop,' he said, 'has served York remarkably well over the years and it would be my hope that the office would continue to serve York to remind the people of the sheer generosity of God and that there is a need for us all to work together to ensure that York is a safe and lively and interesting place to live.'

Since uttering those words, the Archbishop took the courageous decision to quit his high office and take on the less challenging but more spiritual role of the vicar of Ilkley. His conviction and humility in reaching that decision were widely applauded, one commentator comparing him to Cincinnatus, the modest Roman general who had to be almost manhandled from his plough to assume the purple. 'There is a model here for many other grandees in British public life.'

A former high court judge in Idi Amin's Uganda is David Hope's replacement. Fifty-six-year-old Dr John Sentamu, who fled to England to escape the violent regime in his native country to live in England, arrived in York for an exploratory visit in June 2005 and said: 'I'm sure they're going to embrace me. We're straight talkers in Uganda and I'm told they're straight talkers here as well.' Commenting on his appointment, a colleague added: 'You used to send missionaries out to Africa and John is a by-product of that work, but now the church is receiving it back. It's Britain that needs the missionary work today.'

Accompanied by the sound of African drums, Dr Sentamu took up his appointment in a colourful enthronement ceremony in York Minster at the end of November 2005. Dressed in a sky-blue, orange and yellow cope decorated with the twin motifs of a lion and a buffalo in honour of his native tribe, the archbishop quoted a speech by one of his predecessors, Archbishop Ramsey: 'I should love to think of a black Archbishop of York holding a mission here and telling a future generation of the scandal and glory of the Church.' To a tide of laughter and applause that reverberated all round the Minster, the new man in charge added: 'Well, I'm here!'

3

THE MOST HAUNTED CITY IN THE WORLD

Almost every popular treatise on ghosts inclines to the frivolous, stories of spectral dogs, phantoms in irons and sequined dandies with their heads underneath their arms providing a good read and even better theatre. Almost every night of the week, talented actors in period dress will escort visitors round the York streets on so-called 'Ghost Walks' and, if it tickles your fancy, there is even a 'Ghost Cruise'. It is pure entertainment of course and a real boost for tourism, but for a city that has been dubbed by the wonderfully named Ghost Research Foundation International (GRFI) as the most haunted in the world with a total of 504 recorded hauntings, it is also superficial in the extreme. And, in these enlightened times, when we are all just beginning to take a spiritual peek into the Fourth Dimension and beyond, it is woefully hackneyed and not a little patronising. Having stuck in my own two-pennyworth on behalf of the York spirits, I have to hastily record that I do not readily believe in ghosts.

I am as sceptical as the disciple Thomas in accepting that natural laws can be perverted. As a follower of Jesus, he was regularly acquainted with the reality of miracles, and yet even he refused to believe in the Resurrection until he had fingered the holy wounds. Most of us are like Thomas. Only when we have seen with our own eyes and touched with our own hands will we consider the genuineness of something beyond our comprehension. Well, I have to tell you that although I remain sceptical, something happened to me in York that makes me wonder.

Some time ago, I was carrying out research in York library for a piece about the ghosts of Holy Trinity Church in Micklegate. Dressed in white, the shadows of the apparitions regularly flitted across the east window of the church in broad daylight, often during services. The ghosts, which have been almost routinely documented down the years, are supposed to be those of a small girl, her mother and a nurse, passing in the act of visiting the grave of the child's father. Sometimes the ghost of the father is seen as well. Having read all the available material about the phenomenon, I found myself at a loose end. I had a few minutes to spare so I decided to read a book to pass the time. But what should I choose? There were thousands of volumes on the shelves. Without even looking at the title, I selected a book at random and opened the cover. And there before me, pasted on to the flyleaf, was an image of the four ghosts, drawn by a previous

Ghostly images on the flyleaf of
Mr Cobb's private prayer book discovered in
York Reference Library. *(LMA)*

owner of the book in the early eighteenth century. This was a curious coincidence, but what happened next was more curious still.

Shortly after my visit to the library, I was asked by Radio York to give an interview about the ghosts in the churchyard of Holy Trinity. The interview went well in the deserted church grounds and my rendition of the story, which included details of the fortuitous discovery of the drawing, was duly recorded on audio tape. That evening, a rather puzzled reporter telephoned me at home, explaining that the tape had mysteriously picked up the sound of footsteps and the noise of strange laments. A sound engineer checked the recording equipment and the tape for defects but none were found.

Our inherited five senses are the technology of the Dark Ages. This may be a secular and more materialistic age but, at the pioneering fringes, it is also the age of spiritualisation when even quantum physics professors searching for the elusive Theory of Everything bow to the science of mind. Countless people have reported encountering ghosts down the centuries. Perhaps they have been blessed by an intuitive and enlightened way of thinking that opened the pathway to the other side. Perhaps in time we may all tune in to the spirit world. For now, though, most of us will either just scoff or wonder.

Before I escort you on a virtual tour of the dark alleyways and ancient buildings that have witnessed the gruesome history of York, I will pause a while to trim our lamps and ponder on the nature of our quest. By their very natures, ghosts, if they exist, live in a between world of the unresolved. Almost exclusively, they are troubled souls, snatched violently and prematurely from the blood–and–sinew realm of the living to inhabit a tortured staging post of vain regrets and vapours. So in this modern age let us be cautious and not make playthings of phantoms that were once much like us. They are no mere gimcracks to be exploited for the tourist trade. Mock them today and tomorrow you may find your disembodied self, crying out from the place where you died. And the bridge between may be an eternal one, number 505.

The ancient chronicles, the casualty lists and the coroners' reports are crammed full of the names of people who have met untimely ends in York. Thousands have died of plagues and wounds, myriads have succumbed to starvation and neglect, hundreds have committed suicide, countless numbers have been murdered and legions more have been executed in the most barbaric ways imaginable. Millions of the fortunate rest have died in their beds and have gone either this way or that, but at least 500 of the unfortunate others have been stuck in the middle to tread the eternal carousel. With an incomparable history like York's, it is a wonder that there are not thousands more.

York ghosts come in all shapes, sizes and guises from every epoch, Roman, Royalist and Roundhead soldiers taking their places alongside medieval monks, Viking tradesmen, elegantly clad Tudor ladies, railway navvies from the Victorian period and air crew from the Second World War. At the head of the throng are the internationally famous imperial troops who, at the time, appeared in the *Guinness Book of Records* as the oldest recorded spectres in Britain.

People who worked in the Treasurer's House, a large ashlar-built mansion in Minster Yard, had known about the phantom army for decades. Over half a century ago, whispers about its haunted basement had become embedded in local folklore, although employees were reticent to speak out for fear of censure and ridicule. Only years later, when news of the ghosts had been trumpeted worldwide by a visiting tradesman, did one still anonymous woman speak out.

Before the installation of modern central heating in 1953, the Treasurer's House was warmed by a coke boiler. One winter's afternoon, the house caretaker prepared to descend to the fuel store to collect coke. As ever, she was accompanied by her little dog, the shivering animal abruptly halting on the stairs and refusing to descend. Puzzled and agitated, the lady stepped down and entered a passageway, suddenly becoming aware that there was a presence behind her. 'I was petrified', she later admitted. 'I half turned round and saw four or five horses being led by soldiers. They looked completely solid but very weary and very dirty. I couldn't see any legs or feet of horses or men.' After that first apparition, the caretaker saw the dishevelled soldiers two or three times more, describing the men 'leaning on the horses' necks as if they were asleep' after a long and tedious journey. The lady insisted that she had never heard of the Roman ghosts before she saw them. And the story might have been stifled at that point had not a psychically receptive teenager been despatched to the cellar in February 1953.

As an apprentice heating engineer, Harry Martindale (he later became a policeman) got all the mucky jobs and his task was to fit pipes in the Treasurer's House cellar. Busily working away up a short ladder he was distracted by the shrill, far-off sound of a horn. He supposed the blast came from a nearby wireless set and went on with his fixing by the light of an inspection lamp until he saw something that caused him to drop his hammer and fall to the ground. 'A solid object' emerged from the cellar wall at the side of the ladder, a mounted Roman soldier instantly appearing and proceeding to the middle of the room. Behind the soldier was a twenty or so strong contingent of troops marching in pairs, the whole phalanx blocking Harry's escape route down the narrow passageway that led to the stairs. He had no option but to stand, shiver and stare for the few seconds it took for the men to vanish. When they had gone, he scrambled up from the cellar in a terrified state and collapsed into the arms of his workmates. Harry blurted out his incredible story to scorn, ridicule and laughter, but then the curator took the wild-eyed lad aside saying: 'You've seen the Romans!', persuading him to write an account of his encounter immediately, while the details were still fresh in his memory. Harry described his experience and, before long, news of York's latest ghostly visitation hit the headlines, the story reverberating around the world. But what did he see? Bearing in mind that before the event the boy had no knowledge of or interest in Roman history, his descriptions are remarkably detailed.

York Treasurer's House is built on the line of a Roman road. A ghostly phalanx of marching soldiers has been seen in its basement. *(LMA)*

Harry described the small stature of the soldiers and gave details of their dark skins. 'They looked as though they could do with a shave.' The men proceeded sluggishly as though they were exhausted after days of marching, and they were dirty and dusty. They wore roughly dyed, green kilt-like garments above the knee and they were shod in sandals cross-strapped up their shins. On their heads were feather-plumed helmets of burnished metal. Each man was equipped with a gladius worn on the right side, one soldier carrying a horn that Harry noticed was dented. The mounted soldier was said to be riding a carthorse with stout, bushy legs, but the most intriguing description that would eventually corroborate the testimony of the caretaker related to the horses' and the soldiers' legs. In both accounts, they were invisible.

At first historians and academics were sceptical about Harry's description of the soldiers' unusual dress, but subsequent research proved that auxiliary troops, who had been stationed in York towards the end of the Roman period, would have worn such a uniform. The experts were also flummoxed by the obscuring of the legs. The veil was gloriously lifted on this conundrum some years later when excavations in the cellar of the Treasurer's House unearthed the base of a Roman road a foot or so beneath floor level. If you overlay a modern map of York with a detailed archaeological plan of the legionary fortress and its approaches, you will discover that the oft-visited cellar is slap bang in the middle of the Via Decumana.

Moving on from the Treasurer's House, we will attend the vespers call from the nearby Minster and reflect on the spirits that haunt that magnificent place. In 1825, a story was published of an incident in the cathedral that seemed to confirm the existence of heaven itself. A young lady was enjoying an organised tour of the building when a man in distinctive naval costume approached the crowd. He brushed past the lady, who quaked and went white at the sight of her brother, who whispered: 'There is a future state.' For a while, the lady was rigid and silent with fright. Only when she had sufficiently recovered did she confide in her companions the details of a pact made with her brother years earlier. The pair had pledged that whoever died first would appear as a spirit to confirm the existence of a higher realm. Some days later, the lady learnt that her brother had been drowned at sea. Many years later, in the late 1960s, another Minster visitor had a nasty turn. She stood idly examining renovation works that were ongoing at the time, when she was accosted by a strangely attired workman in an odd hat. 'I carved that,' he boasted, pointing to an intricately worked figure in stone. Before the dumbfounded woman could catch her breath, the vision had disappeared.

On then to another building that oozes history, the elegant mansion known as King's Manor in Exhibition Square with its resident coterie of ghosts. The building began life as the abbot's house attached to the adjacent St Mary's Abbey. A displaced monk, forever disgruntled at his eviction by the King at the time of the Dissolution, stalks the corridors. Alongside him is a companion female spirit, allegedly that of Anne Boleyn. Elegantly dressed in a green Tudor costume, the phantom carries a posy of red roses. Outside the mansion, a ravaged knot of troubled souls emits the blood-curdling sounds of a primitive field hospital. During the Battle of Marston Moor on 2 July 1644, Roundhead casualties were brought to the courtyard for surgery, and sometimes their tortured screams rent the night air.

Follow me now to what is for me the most bloodstained spot in the whole of York. Clifford's Tower, part of the original York Castle, was used as a macabre place of exposition for the display of executed men of rank, the body of the Yorkshire patriot Robert Aske, who led the Pilgrimage of Grace in 1536, hanging from the battlements for months. But it is an infamous and much earlier event of 1190 that will forever haunt Clifford's Tower. During the twelfth century, England was guilty of anti-Semitism. The Jews were persecuted, particularly as the nation's bankers at a time when loans were needed to fund the Third Crusade. Riots broke out in London and spread to York, and Jewish businesses and homes in the city were attacked and ransacked, over a hundred terrified Jews taking refuge in Clifford's Tower. Besieged by an angry mob, the Jewish leaders, in an act that hideously matched the mass suicide at Masada in AD 70, killed their women and children and then turned their knives on themselves. Some traitors escaped from the tower and pleaded with the besiegers for clemency but they too were butchered, the incensed mob storming the Minster and burning holy books, deeds and financial records in the nave to finally expunge their debts.

An intense melancholy has emanated from this place ever since and, some time after the tower was rebuilt in stone, red stains began to appear on the blockwork, prompting suggestions that it was weeping with 'Jews' blood'. Scientific analysis has subsequently revealed that the stains are a form of iron oxide, but oddly, no other stone from the same quarry has the same impurities. In old chronicles there is also reference to the spontaneous appearance of a red patch of earth at the bottom of one of the tower's staircases. Explained as a rare form of fungus, it was repeatedly dug up, only to regrow overnight. In 1682, Clifford's Tower was recommended for demolition but it still survives and continues to weave its doleful spell. In recent times, one lady has, under hypnosis, suggested that she was a reincarnated Jewess who was there on the terrible night of 16 March 1190. She vividly recalled intimate details of her ordeal, suggesting that she escaped with her family to the sanctuary of a crypt in the nearby St Mary's Church in Castlegate. According to detailed records no such crypt ever existed but then in 1975, workmen who were excavating the church foundations stumbled on a subterranean space that matched the lady's description precisely.

So far in this chapter we have concentrated on the spirits that haunt York's grander public places, but they also inhabit more prosaic buildings of course, almost every pub in the city having its own resident ghost. Across the river from Clifford's Tower, the Cock and Bottle in Skeldergate is reputedly haunted by George Villiers, the second Duke of Buckingham. A seventeenth-century womaniser, playboy, politician, poet and roué who inspired the nursery rhyme about 'Georgie Porgie' after his fall from power in 1673, the Duke once lived in a mansion on the site of the pub. After his disgrace, he retired to a farmhouse in Kirkbymoorside and wasted away, begging in the height of a fever to be taken to his beloved York to spend his last days. But he was too ill to travel and died in the country. Afterwards, as befitting his rank, he was taken to Westminster Abbey for burial in an unmarked grave. He was a reprobate in life and he continues his scandalous ways in death. Fittingly, though, he appears only to women. Successive licensees have reported a pervading evil, sudden and unaccountable drops in

The Golden Fleece claims to be the most haunted inn in York. *(LMA)*

temperature and regular sightings of a disturbed and agitated man with dark curly hair and a wide-brimmed hat who has an aversion to crucifixes. The apparitions are sometimes accompanied by the sound of a heavy door being moved. Pictures have fallen from walls and cutlery has mysteriously disappeared, only to reappear some time later in the most unlikely of places. The one aspect that really affirms the Duke's identity, however, is his licentious preference for women. A former landlady recalls one frightening and embarrassing moment with a shiver and a smile. Away from the bar, she was taking a shower upstairs when she heard the bathroom door open. In walked a strange man. His large outline was clearly visible through the frosted glass of the shower cubicle. The man approached the shower and the lady screamed, alerting her husband. He came running as the spectre fled towards the attic. A frantic search of the attic proved fruitless. But it appears the landlady got away lightly, some ladies alleging lewd behaviour that might normally be regarded as indecent assault. Other phantoms afflict the Black Swan on Peasholme Green, the York Arms in High Petergate and the Old Star Inn in Petergate, the groans of wounded soldiers taken there after the Battle of Marston Moor still haunting its cellars. It's to that barren killing ground just seven miles west of the city centre that we journey next. There marches another phantom army.

On a dark, misty evening in November 1932, commercial traveller Tom Horner was driving his car from York towards Green Hammerton and had just passed Marston Moor railway station when he had to pull over to allow an oncoming coach to pass along the narrow lane. In the passenger seat was Tom's friend Arthur Wright, who became immediately aware of a group of bedraggled men in front of the car on the verge. 'Look out!' he shouted, urging Tom to slow down. Picked out in the headlights about 20 yards from the vehicle were three figures all distinctively attired as Cavaliers. They wore shoulder-length hair under cockaded wide-brimmed hats, swirling cloaks and long boots. Shaken, the two men leapt from the car and decided to investigate, but although they searched the by now deserted road, they found nothing. Thirty-six years later, in 1968, a car full of tourists who were new to the area found themselves lost in the same spot. They too reported seeing apparitions, described at the time as 'half-a-dozen tramps', like 'exhausted campaigners'. And the sightings did not end there. From time to time apparitions have been seen ten miles or so west of Marston Moor in the Forest of Knaresborough. On that bloody July day in 1644, some 4,000 royalist soldiers died, Cromwell pursuing scores of the Marquis of Newcastle's infantry west from the battlefield and cutting them down as they ran. Some observers have described seeing a detachment of men in white uniforms led by a sword-wielding general in a scarlet tunic. Could these be the ghosts of the famous Whitecoats and their commander who were cruelly butchered that day?

York, then, has hundreds of ghosts, and the GRFI is still counting. So go on a 'Ghost Walk' if you must but afterwards visit the brooding Marston Moor alone at night and stand by the monument to the fallen. You will find that there is nothing frivolous about that.

4

THE MINSTERMEN

Football – the beautiful game. The greatest sport in the world is like an enchantress. Captivating and exciting, she draws you in breathless with anticipation of that ultimate moment. She tantalises and torments you and takes you to the brink, leaving you quivering and shrieking on the ecstatic edge, that addictive cliff compelling the unrequited you, time after time, into her arms. The Goddess of the Goal leads the line at Old Trafford, Stamford Bridge and Highbury, her lesser acolytes haunting the penalty areas at Bloomfield Road and Bootham Crescent, the home of the Minstermen and York City Soccer Club. But wherever the white ball flies, these sirens have the recruiting talents of a Dracula's virgins' kiss. Impassioned and addicted, dads at schoolboy fixtures, bucket-and-sponge men at non-league games and fans of Manchester United are forever compelled to wear the scarf, dreaming of that consummate shout of 'GOAL!'

Goals were the dream of the founders of York City Football Club. The club was formed in 1922, building on an appetite for a free-for-all game that had been played in the city for several centuries. Although the rumbustious and un-disciplined sport was frowned on by the authorities, football was nevertheless popular in York and energetic youngsters from both sides of the social divide joined in the fun. In 1565, Christopher Dobson, a pupil from St Peter's School, found an unusual pitch for his kick-about and was charged with other boys that 'they have plaied at the foote ball within the cathedral church of Yorke'. As an example, Dobson was put in the stocks and given six strokes of the birch rod on his buttocks. The games continued and, in the winter of 1608, when the River Ouse was frozen solid, there are records of a football match on the ice. Early discussions about creating a professional club in the city were held in the Blue Bell public house in Fossgate, its landlord George Robinson becoming one of the club's first directors.

Raising £2,000, the directors bought 8 acres of land in Heslington Lane, Fulfordgate, on a site now occupied by the University. The ground, which was first known as Gate Fulford and then Fulfordgate, was endowed with second-hand open stands purchased from York Race Committee. An old army hut served as modest dressing rooms. York City became members of the Midlands League, their inaugural match being played against Mansfield Town on Wednesday 20 September 1922. Just seven years later, in 1929, following considerable ground improvements, the club was granted entry into Division Three North of the Football League as a replacement for Ashington. Prompted by poor attendances, exacerbated by inadequate transport links to the city, the club was moved to a new, more conveniently situated leased ground at Bootham Crescent in time for the 1932/3 season. Since then, successes and failures, promotions, relegations, applications for re-election and financial catastrophes have tested fans' belief in the Muses to the limit. In 2002, to the surprise and disgust of many, the team of the 'City Reds' became York City Soccer Club, ditching the word 'football' from their title – the first professional club in the country to do so – as an initiative by flashy new chairman John Batchelor. Within six months of his takeover, Batchelor, who made some of his pile through developing the theme park at Flamingoland near Malton, was accused of asset stripping and in April 2002, a secret deal was concocted between his company BCH and national house builder Persimmon for the sale of the Bootham Crescent ground, conditional on vacant possession. Outraged loyal fans set up a trust to help thwart the proposals as a planning application was lodged late in 2002 seeking the erection of ninety-three houses on the site. The fight was on, the expiration of the BCH lease in June 2004 really concentrating minds. The Minstermen, meanwhile, continued to play not very inspiring football that at the end of the 2003/4 season led, after seventy-five years in league football, to the ignominious drop. For the moment, York City are in the doldrums of the Nationwide Conference League, although their long-term survival at Bootham Crescent now looks secure.

After a league history marked by inconsistency, the Minstermen's finest hour, perhaps, came in the 1983/4 season when they became the first club in Football League history to reach the magical 100 points. That momentous season they finally opened their display cabinet, winning the Division Four championship by an astonishing 15 points clear of Doncaster Rovers – the biggest margin ever. They also set several new club records – most wins, 31, most away wins, 13, most league doubles, 11 and most goals, 96, using a squad of only sixteen players. For once, the fans were delirious, the *Yorkshire Evening Press* eulogising the champions in the headline: TEAM OF THE CENTURY. The City of York joined in the celebrations, laying on a civic reception, thousands of supporters lining the route of the cavalcade to a banquet in the Mansion House. As league champions, York City won £8,000 in league prize money. To mark their singular achievement in reaching a ton of goals, league sponsors Canon added a further £1,000 to the purse.

On paper, the achievements of 1983/4 represent the acme of the club's success, but every supporter knows that true glory, at least for the smaller clubs denied entry into European competitions, comes from success in what is regarded as the supreme knockout tournament in world football. 'We're going to toast each other from that silver cup' boasts a verse from a rollicking anthem from the repertoire of my own team – Leeds United. Well, little York City, just a tantalising twice in their existence, almost got their smackers on the FA Cup.

Over the years, City have earned for themselves a deserved reputation as cup giant-killers and have won their way to appearances in both the quarter- and semi-finals. In their first league season in 1929/30 they held Newcastle to a draw in the third round, only narrowly losing the replay at Fulfordgate before nearly 13,000 spectators. The following year, the team entertained Sheffield United after another third-round draw, losing again, to the disappointment of a second bumper crowd. But the real excitement came in 1937/8 when, after a low-key start in the first two rounds, they got within a whisker of the semi-finals.

Their first match was at home to Halifax Town in November 1937. Despite a spirited start, Town took a shock lead with a well-taken goal in the seventh minute, City rallying with a Spooner shot that whizzed over the bar. The rest of the half was dominated by the home side but they failed to capitalise on their superiority and at half time they were in deficit to that single goal. But they came out fighting, forcing a number of corners. Spooner's cross was soon flicked on by Baines to Hughes who headed home in the fifty-second minute. An end-to-end battle raged for the remaining half hour and although City managed to scramble the ball into the net, courtesy of the ever-probing Spooner, the goal was disallowed for handball. The match ended 1–1 and the replay was held at the Shay ground in Halifax just a few days later.

In rather foggy conditions, the defences took charge in dour early exchanges, but gradually Halifax forced a succession of fine saves. Against the run of play, having survived a fierce Halifax drive deflected off the crossbar, York took the lead, a fine pass from Comrie to Baines, who took the ball in his stride, leading to a tremendous goal that beat the keeper 'all ends up'. In the second half, the lively Baines tormented the Halifax defence and the match ended in a deserved victory for York City, the outstanding Wharton, Wass, Legge, Hughes, Comrie and Baines taking the honours. The jubilant Yorkshire team was drawn in the next round away to Division Three South battlers Clapton Orient and in December, they made the long journey to Leytonstone to play their first ever game in London.

After a fiercely contested start, City were two goals down by the thirty-seventh minute, the sizeable contingent of supporters, who had travelled 200 miles and braved the winter weather, becoming subdued at half time. But City rallied at the whistle and threw everything into attack, the Clapton defence somehow keeping a clean sheet with just fifteen minutes to go. Yorkshire caps were twisted in agony until Scott tapped the ball home after a scramble in the goalmouth in the seventy-fifth minute and it was game on, the City players pushing everyone forward, team captain Legge at full back inspiring his players to one final effort. With only four minutes left, Spooner broke free on the left wing and centred for Comrie to score a magnificent equaliser.

The return game was played in difficult conditions. A blanket of snow had to be removed from the Bootham Crescent pitch and 10 tons of sand were spread and rolled to allow the match to start. But City started brightly and were 'all over' their southern opponents in the first fifteen minutes, twice hitting the woodwork. Clapton resolutely held on until half time. In the second half, the home team pressed forward with determination and their attacks paid off in the seventy-eighth minute, Scott taking a free kick just outside the penalty area and Baines deflecting the ball to Hughes, who hammered in from close range. For only the fifth time in the history of the club, York City were in the hat for the third round of the FA Cup, an excited journalist in the *Northern Echo* reporting: 'Both sides gave a clean, clever and exhilarating display that will go down in the annals of Bootham Crescent as one of the best of Cup matches.'

Holding back the excited crowds during one of the 1938 cup-ties. *(York & County Press)*

There was both relief and nervousness when details of the draw came through. 'Number 6 – York City (ah!) – will play number 15 – Coventry City (oh!)' At the time, Coventry were pressing for promotion and were joint leaders of the Second Division having lost only two of their twenty-two league games. And York could not have had a worse preparation for the game of their lives. Just before the big day, in a morale-depressing match, they were 'slugged' 0–5 in a home league game with Rochdale. And woe and more woe. Talismanic skipper Legge was out through injury.

A record crowd of nearly 14,000 packed into Bootham Crescent for an all-action match that saw two goals within the first ten minutes. Spooner's opener for the Minstermen was cruelly wiped out, the courageous and usually safe-handed Wharton spilling a corner-kicked cross into his net. Both sides poured on the pressure and York began to prevail, and in the twenty-third minute they scored again, Comrie passing to Hughes, who smashed a fine shot net-bound. With their tails up, York continued to surge forward and they slammed in another super goal in the thirty-third minute, Duckworth's long cross-field path to Earl allowing the winger to make it 2–0 at half time.

In the first twenty minutes of the second half, Coventry rallied and played some brilliant football, scoring in the sixty-second minute. After that it was a rip-roaring contest. In the last frantic quarter, Earl was carried off unconscious after a collision with a defender and Wass was left with blood streaming down his face from a cut head following another tussle. York were ragged and depleted, but their supporters roared them on to victory, a standing ovation at the end applauding a giant-killing act that reverberated around the city for weeks. But what would that little black bag bring next?

Another home tie! The opponents this time though were in a different league. Seasoned campaigners West Bromwich Albion were in the First Division. But then as now the maxim was 'the cup's a great leveller' and York were in optimistic mood.

There was a carnival atmosphere in York, both teams enjoying entertainment at the Empire Theatre on the night before the match. The Cup is unique in fostering bonhomie and tomfoolery between rival fans, and on the morning of the game, all roads, clogged with noisy supporters sporting scarves, banners, rattles and mascots, led to the ground. It was the sort of unforgettable day when dads turn to their sons and say: 'Enjoy the match son 'cause you might not see the like at the Crescent again.' Well, nearly seventy years on, I talked to a lifelong City Red who was there that day in short pants and he still remembers every kick.

Nearly 19,000 fans saw history in the making, some climbing precariously on to the stand roof to get a better view. City made a lively start but against the run of play, Albion took a fortuitous twenty-third minute lead, after a cruel deflection. But York responded well. Denied two calls for penalties, they pressed on and at half time they were unlucky to be behind.

At the resumption, Albion came close, Wharton making a tremendous save. Then Baines got his reward. A third trip in the area and a deafening shout of 'Penalty!' led to an equaliser from the spot, a gleeful Baines doing the business. Roared on, City surged forward to assault the Albion goal. Then Pindar went off injured and ten-man City succumbed on the break to a second Albion strike in the sixty-eighth minute. And the seconds ticked agonisingly by. Another York attack was repulsed. City fans groaned and hastily consulted their watches. Just six minutes to the whistle and the gallant cup run looked spent. Then a glimmer of hope. City were awarded a free kick, our lad and his dad clasping their prayerful hands together in supplication. And a miracle happened. Pinder crossed from the right and Baines headed home to ecstasy and delirium. Incredibly, York City were drawing with three times FA Cup winners West Bromwich Albion 2–2. Blow now! Blow now for a replay! But to misquote Kenneth Wolstenholme's famous phrase: 'They thought it was all over! Well, it was then!' With only three minutes left on the clock, hero of the hour Baines bundled an Earl corner kick into the net. The Albion players disputed the goal for handball but the referee had no doubts – 3–2!

There was pandemonium at the end, hundreds of spectators pouring on to the pitch to salute the team that had, for the first time ever, beaten First Division opposition. The win was heralded in the local press, the *Yorkshire Evening Press* headlining the victory as YORK'S BIGGEST FOOTBALL THRILL. But who next? Bring on First Division title contenders and fancied cup favourites Middlesbrough. Surely the fairy tale could not continue?

As fans caught their breath, journalists soberly examined the vital statistics of a David-and-Goliath contest that promised annihilation for the upstarts from Division Three. City were written off as a £50 team, pundits disparagingly pointing out that apart from the £50 paid to Sheffield United for the services of Peter Spooner, the entire team had cost nothing in transfer fees. But fans were assured that the write-offs would go down fighting.

The whole of Yorkshire was agog as the match day approached, the directors of City steadfastly refusing to transfer the tie to their rivals bigger stadium at Ayresome Park. As a thoughtful concession to fans, the directors also refused Middlesbrough's request to double ticket prices, although entry charges were increased across the board, the cost of main stand seats rising to 7s 6d. Undaunted, fans clamoured for tickets and ground capacity was increased, 1,000 tons of banking material providing extra space behind both goals. On the big day, the bus and railway stations were thronged with people and all approaches to the ground were clogged with cars and long cavalcades of excited fans, mounted police helping to keep order. Some lucky constables were also stationed on top of the stand roof to prevent a dangerous repetition of the climbing that had occurred at the start of the Albion game. An unchanged City lined up to face a Middlesbrough team that ominously included a highly rated inside-forward – Wilf Mannion.

Having lost the toss, City had to play against a troublesome wind and they made heavy weather of it in the first quarter, although they matched the opposition in every department and twenty minutes elapsed before Wharton was called upon to make his first save. Gradually, though, they started playing good football, with Baines and Earl both going close. Mannion, a star of the future, came close but, tackle-for-tackle, the underdogs matched their opponents and it was 0–0 at half time.

With the wind now in their favour, City stepped up a gear and in the fifty-third minute, the impressive Comrie passed the ball to Spooner who, in a heart-stopping moment, let loose a magnificent left-foot drive to open the score. The crowd went bananas, screaming again in the next minute when a fierce Baines shot was parried by the keeper, Spooner heading the rebound over the bar. Far from protecting their lead, the irrepressible City besieged the Middlesbrough lines and at the end of a frantic 90 minutes, they won by that precious goal. The crowd of nearly 24,000 roared with wonder and delight, upwards of 5,000 fans dashing on to the pitch at the final whistle to mob their heroes. York City, a league side for only nine seasons and just sixteen years old, had, amazingly, reached the quarter-finals of the FA Cup.

By the time of the next draw, York City were making national headlines, one newspaper covering the next Yorkshire clash with First Division opposition

Huddersfield Town sagely reporting that the 'eyes of the country are on York City'. The Minstermen spent a few days unwinding in Scarborough before the epic clash as cup fever took hold, one of the greatest days in the club's history – Saturday 5 March 1938 – dawning bright and clear. Spectators converged on Bootham Crescent and all the turnstiles were locked before the kick-off, an all-time record crowd of 28,000 fans giving both teams a rapturous reception. In the VIP seats were the Lord and Lady Mayoress of York and the Foreign Secretary, Viscount Halifax, York's MP. For the fourth successive cup tie, City fielded an unchanged side.

From the first pass, the match was fast and furious, both defences dominating. The first half ended goalless but as soon as the whistle blew for the second period, the York goal was assailed, Wharton making a magnificent save to keep his side in the game. In the seventy-first minute, a move that has since become part of City folklore stopped the heart of every Tyke in the ground. Earl centred from the right wing, the advancing Spooner cheekily heading the ball net-bound over the advancing keeper. With the salute 'Goal!' already rising from 20,000 larynxes, a frantic defender scooped the ball away and York fans choked, Huddersfield storming back with an assault of their own. For once, Wharton was beaten by a fine shot but the ball struck the crossbar and bounced to safety. In a tense and dramatic final few minutes, City forced four corners, Wass saving the day at the other end with a goal-line clearance of his own. Honours were shared that day, both defences cancelling out concerted attacks. For City, Pinder was outstanding, Huddersfield centre-half Young keeping Baines in check. Mightily applauded by every fan in the country, plucky City could hardly comprehend what came next, the name of their side going into the hat for the semi-final draw: 'Aston Villa will play Preston North End and York City or Huddersfield will play Sunderland.' First, York needed to beat Huddersfield in the replay, but they were just three more wins from immortality.

The teams met at Leeds Road on 9 March before a stupendous crowd of over 58,000. An exodus of fans left York by train, bus and private car but the congestion in Huddersfield was immense, some fans abandoning their vehicles in a frantic effort to get to the ground on time. The City manager, Tom Mitchell, again fielded an unchanged side: Wharton, Pinder, Barrett, Duckworth, Wass, Hathway, Earl, Hughes, Baines, Comrie and Spooner.

City struggled against a contrary wind and a first-half bombardment by the excellent Town and managed to keep the score 0–0 by half time. The rearguard action continued into the second half, but in the sixty-eighth minute, Town scored following a scrappy goalmouth scramble. The never-say-die Yorkshire spirit kept City going to the end, Comrie almost grabbing an equaliser with a back-header. City lost by the single goal that day, so ending a most remarkable cup run. York City gained only pride and honour in a stirring defeat, the *Northern Echo* publishing a reverberating headline: YORK CITY'S RUN ENDED – BUT NO REGRETS – TEAM HAVE SHED LIMELIGHT ON THE NORTHERN SECTION. The football press joined in the eulogies, describing 'A glorious chapter in York City's history – the victories against teams from every section of the Football League – the crowds – the receipts – the almost world-wide publicity.'

A good crowd watching the Minstermen in a 1948/9 home game. *(York & County Press)*

The journal went on to record: 'City supporters will never forget 1937/8. It may be years and years before a York City team equals the Cup performance of the present side.' And it was – seventeen years to be precise. Huddersfield Town meanwhile went on to Wembley, losing the FA Cup Final to Preston North End.

By 1954, spasmodic form and mediocre performances on the field had taken the shine off City's finest hour and few fans were hopeful of an improvement. Eventually, though, the introduction of new players such as Arthur Bottom, who made his debut in August 1954 and went on to become the most prolific goal scorer in club history, ensured a change in fortune. Domestically, the 1954/5 season went well, the team finishing a most respectable fourth in Division Three North. But it was in the FA Cup that City achieved everlasting glory, becoming the first ever Third Division club to play in an FA Cup semi-final replay.

The campaign began prosaically enough with a home match against weak Midland League opposition Scarborough. A complacent City, over-confident after an unbeaten run of ten league matches, nearly fell at the first hurdle, an enthusiastic early display by the Seasiders leading to first blood in the twenty-fourth minute. A shaken City equalised early in the second half but they

struggled to rally from a second setback, only clinching the tie with a third goal
five minutes from the end. In the second round, the victors drew unknown
quantity Dorchester Town of the Western League.

Only 150 supporters made the long journey to Dorset, the band of the Dorset
Regiment playing 'On Ilkla Moor Baht 'At' in honour of the visitors. The home
side took a shock lead and rattled City with some excellent football, the mercurial
Bottom coming to the rescue shortly before the interval with a fine goal. During
the second period, City shrugged off their lethargy and turned on the skill,
scoring three times in just ten minutes, Bottom completing his hat-trick and
Wilkinson netting with a header. Town pulled a goal back from the penalty spot,
but Fenton completed the comprehensive win by scoring near the end, sealing a
2–5 victory for York. Magnanimous in defeat, the Dorchester secretary made a
prophetic statement: 'I pity any First Division team who meet these continental
Yorkshiremen.' Spectator David Jack, a former England international, added
some knowledgeable words of his own: 'York played some really brilliant football
and performed like world-beaters in a devastating spell.' The minnows had been
disposed of, so bring on the sharks.

The third-round draw uncorked the champagne bottle good and proper, the
razzmatazz of the FA Cup seeing famous Division One glamour boys Blackpool
drawn at home to City in what promised to be a cracking match. Eighteen months
earlier, Blackpool had triumphed over Bolton 4–3 in a match that has gone down
in history as the 'Matthews Final' and the maestro was still there alongside other
legendary teammates – internationals Mortensen, Taylor, Johnston and Farm. It
was a tall order for City, and the contingent of 5,000 fans that made the tortuous
journey over the Pennines on that cold January day in 1955 knew it.

City manager Jimmy McCormick had resigned earlier in the season, chief
trainer Tom Lockie ably stepping into the breach and developing a characteristic
'skilful, close-passing, push-and-run' style of game. Now referred to as the
'Happy Wanderers' in allusion to a popular song of the period, City quickly
adopted their now familiar tactics and, after weathering early Blackpool pressure,
they started to dominate before a 26,000 packed crowd. Crucially, Howe, with
intelligent positional play and timely tackling, kept Matthews quiet, the whole
half-back line rising to the occasion with some great play. And in the thirty-
seventh minute they struck gold. Storey sent a speculative cross into the
Blackpool penalty area, Farm misjudged the flight of the ball and it crossed the
line. The goal sparked further attacks and Blackpool finished the half lucky to be
only one goal down.

Stung into action, Blackpool began the second half strongly but City held firm,
even though they suffered an injury to Hughes who spent the rest of the match
limping out on the wing. With no thought of protecting their lead, they kept the
Blackpool keeper busy, further denting the Seasiders' pride in the seventieth
minute when a perfect through ball from Wilkinson was despatched by Fenton
from 12 yards. Blackpool desperately sought to close the gap and with only twelve
minutes left, they were awarded a controversial penalty. Forgan in the City goal
punched clear and the Yorkshiremen finished strongly at the end, reaching
another milestone for the club. They were the first team to beat First Division

opposition away from home. The press celebrated the famous victory in skittish mood. The headline in the *Sunday Express*, OH BLACKPOOL – WHAT A YORKER!, was matched with the *Northern Echo*'s GIANTKILLING ACT WAS A TRIUMPH OF SKILL. The *Sports Press* chirped: 'Five thousand fans certainly did like to be beside the seaside', heaping special accolades on the efforts of City's Howe, Stewart and Brown. After the match, the victors were regaled at a champagne reception in a Clitheroe hotel. The *Pathé News* recorded the match highlights for transmission in cinemas nationwide, later presenting a souvenir copy of their film to City skipper Phillips.

The draw for the fourth round brought City back to earth. They were drawn away again and paired with the best amateur side in the land. And Bishop Auckland were no pushover. They had won the FA Amateur Cup a record number of times and had a posse of amateur internationals in their squad, including skipper Bob Hardisty who had captained Great Britain's team in the 1948 Olympics. The all-ticket match was billed as the 'Clash of the Giant Killers' and the 'Bishops versus the Minstermen'.

Before a 15,000 crowd, City opened the scoring with a goal by Storey in an evenly contested first period, Bishop Auckland equalising in a thrilling first half. The end-to-end football continued in the second period but, gradually, class told. Although the Bishops continued to be dangerous on the break, City took charge, that man Bottom popping up to seal the tie in the seventy-ninth minute. Then, in the eithty-fourth minute, Hughes was tripped and Bottom made it 3–1 from the spot. This time, the *Sports Press* was less whimsical, its headline recording AMATEURS ECLIPSED BY METHODICAL FOOTBALL.

Hearing the news of the fifth-round draw, City players experienced a mixture of relief, elation and nervousness. They were drawn at home against the mighty Tottenham Hotspur from the First Division. It was enough to make the knees quake. The Spurs had a star-studded line-up that included the recent £30,000 signing from Aston Villa, Danny Blanchflower. They also had Alf Ramsey, who would later manage England's World Cup winning team and Mel Hopkins, Tony Marchi, Eddie Baily, Len Duquemin and George Robb. In opposition, City would field a side that boasted four part-time players. Sid Storey worked in a coalmine near Barnsley. Billy Fenton was a York draughtsman. Gordon Brown was a storeman in Mansfield and Norman Wilkinson cobbled shoes in West Stanley. How would they cope against the Brylcreem Boys of London? City fans were keen to find out, and all 21,000 tickets for the game were quickly snapped up.

Bootham Crescent ground staff worked through the night to clear the pitch of ice and the teams kicked off with snow falling. In the eleventh minute, Spurs opened the scoring. Stung into action, City stormed back and forced a number of corners. And, roared on by the fans, they netted twice in two glorious minutes. Fenton broke free from Ramsey on a surging cross-field run and cleverly back-heeled to Hughes. He crossed an inch-perfect ball to Hughes, who headed home. In the next attack, Spurs were ripped apart again. The jinking Bottom beat two defenders and passed to Wilkinson, who unleashed a stinging drive. This was knocked down by the keeper and ran loose to Fenton who gleefully drove it home. You could hear the applause in Leeds. And City kept up the pressure until the half-time whistle, Fenton's pace causing all sorts of problems to the Spurs' defence.

Spurs came out fighting after the break and nearly scored from a header, Robb clearing off the line. And still the home side surged forward, both Fenton and Bottom coming close. Forgan made one fine save to keep the visitors out but with just ten minutes left, City were in control. Then in the eightieth minute came a moment to savour. Fenton out-played Ramsey again and crossed for Wilkinson to score a third gaol for City. In the final few minutes, only a magnificent save at full stretch by the Tottenham keeper kept Fenton from his hat-trick. At the final whistle it was 3–1 to the Minstermen and the jubilant crowd swarmed on to the pitch to celebrate a victory that is arguably the best in the entire history of the club. City became the first Northern Section club to reach the last eight of the competition twice, having at last equalled the feat of their counterparts seventeen years earlier. The newsstands nationwide were abuzz:

CITY GIANTKILLERS DO IT AGAIN – SPURS OUTPLAYED FROM START TO FINISH OF THRILLER, reported the *Sports Press*.
NO FLUKE: IT MIGHT HAVE BEEN SIX! trumpeted the *Daily Express*.
YORK CITY LOOKED LIKE 1950 SPURS SIDE commented the *News Chronicle*.
SPURS RIDE ENDS AT YORK bannered the *Sunday Express*.
The county's own daily, the *Yorkshire Post*, succinctly summed up the achievement with A FOOTBALLING TRIUMPH.

The red-faced Tottenham players were generous in defeat. 'York's standard of play left us speechless', admitted Danny Blanchflower. 'They were better in all departments. They played so well we could not blame the state of the pitch. I think they would have won whatever the conditions.' 'York were the better team and deserved to win', acknowledged Alf Ramsey. 'They showed they could play good football on the difficult pitch.' And under the NO FLUKE headline, the *Daily Express* chief soccer correspondent wrote this: 'The humiliation, the unmistakable Cup blitz of London's soccer aristocrats was achieved by a team who played Spurs' own immaculate stylish soccer but played it more quickly, more accurately and played it with more sense of urgency and spirit.' Straight-talking trainer Tom Lockie added the most telling and laconic comment of them all: 'We have no special plan. We try to play correct football and depend a lot on defensive cover. If one man is beaten, a team-mate doubles back to cover him. There is only one ball on the field. One side cannot have it all the time. We make sure we get most of it.'

The further you go in the FA Cup journey the more exciting it gets, and hearts were all aflutter when the announcement of the sixth-round ties was made. City were drawn away to Notts County of the Second Division. County were not as formidable as Spurs, but their recent form had impressively seen off Middles-brough, Sheffield Wednesday and the mighty Chelsea, who ended up as champions of the First Division. The mood was one of respect but quiet confidence.

City were cheered on by over 11,000 fans, the exodus from York being the biggest in the history of the club. Over 47,000 spectators packed into the Meadow

Lane ground, setting a new capacity record for County. Still giddy from the success of the previous rounds, the Yorkshire contingent expected an exciting match, but the game was generally a dour contest dominated by excellent defensive work by both sides. Both teams netted, only to be ruled offside either side of half time and fans had to wait until the seventy-eighth minute for the deadlock to be broken by Bottom. His historic goal was his thirty-first of the season, equally the club's scoring record.

The 'Happy Wanderers' were drowned in a sea of fans, a journalist in the *Sports Press* later reporting: 'Amidst scenes which I have never seen equalled before in a football ground, the amazing York City team could hardly fight its way to the dressing room after its 1–0 victory over Notts County.' Meanwhile, back in an expectant York, there was wild cheering as a loudspeaker announcement interrupted play in the York Rugby League match at Clarence Street. There were similar scenes of jubilation in local cinemas when the result was flashed on screens, hundreds of other people, who had been glued to their radios all afternoon, rushing out into the streets to share the good news. The scenes of celebration in York that Saturday evening were described as quite incredible, publicans doing a roaring trade. Fourteen specially chartered trains pulled into the station at intervals, thousands of rosetted, scarf-waving, bell-ringing, rattle-turning fans, joining hundreds more in the concourse for an impromptu party that lasted until midnight. By 9.30 p.m., a crowd of several hundred fans waited expectantly for the team coach to arrive in Blossom Street, a police escort leading the heroes to a celebration dinner in the Victoria Hotel. That Sunday morning, York rose to a collective hangover as the telegrams continued to pour in, marking a red-letter footballing achievement in the city that has never been equalled.

The draw for the semi-finals made scary reading. Manchester City were matched against Sunderland at Villa Park. York City had to overcome the winners of the replay between Huddersfield Town and Newcastle at Hillsborough, a victory for the Magpies preventing an all-Yorkshire clash.

Saturday 26 March 1955 was the most important day in the history of York City and, as far as fans were concerned, the most memorable sporting occasion of the century. Crowd capacity at Hillsborough for the all-ticket game was set at 65,000 and every ticket was sold, touts doing great business before the match at vastly inflated prices. Some 21,000 fans – one fifth of the city's population – travelled from York by road and rail in dismal weather. Over one hundred buses were charted and British Rail laid on twenty special trains, many other fans arriving by car. A persistent downpour and news that Sid Storey had failed a fitness test and was sidelined failed to dampen the Yorky spirit and, as the bells in the Minster tolled for 3 p.m., the match was begun.

The teams lined up as follows:

York City: Forgan, Phillips, Howe, Brown, Stewart, Spence, Hughes, Bottom, Wilkinson, McNab and Fenton.

Newcastle United: Simpson, Cowell, Batty, Scoular, Stokoe, Casey, White, Davies, Keeble, Milburn and Mitchell.

After incessant rain, the Hillsborough pitch was heavy and sticky and, as the teams ran out, it was still pouring, a Niagara of applause and chanting surging over the ground. Back in 1955, before legislation set crowd capacities and introduced mandatory safety measures, those fans were packed in like sardines to within inches of both goals and touchlines. Imagine then the atmosphere on that wet afternoon. Some idea of the cauldron of noise generated by the 65,000 voices can be judged by the comments of Richard Ulyatt, an experienced *Yorkshire Post* sportswriter who was present that day. He reported on many games at Wembley and Hampden Park but he described the thunderous roar that greeted the teams as the most deafening he had ever heard.

Newcastle struck first, an early goal by Keeble in the fourteenth minute beating Forgan. Undaunted, City roared back, only a last-ditch tackle on Fenton by Scoular keeping them out. Keeble nearly scored again for the Magpies, then Stokoe was robbed in midfield by Bottom. Leaving every defender in his wake, he ran 30 yards, Simpson desperately leaving his line to intercept. Bottom swerved and slammed the ball into the empty net. Celebratory cartwheels were unknown in 1955, but Bottom foreshadowed the tomfoolery by thirty seasons by jigging, broad-faced, all the way back to the half-way line pursued by excited teammates. Clearly rattled, Newcastle held on until half time.

Forty-five minutes of furious football had churned up the pitch and after the interval, both sides found the going tough. Newcastle pressed hard but City resisted strongly, inspired by skipper Phillips. A rock in defence, he shackled United's talented forward Mitchell. Towards the final whistle, City finished the stronger side and in the eightieth minute came one of those 'if only' moments that is still talked about in York. There was a sliding scramble in the Newcastle penalty area, Bottom soaring above the mire to head for goal. The despairing keeper cleared off the line with a one-handed save. But had the ball crossed the line? Twenty-one thousand City fans thought it had but, amid wild scenes, the referee blew for a foul and awarded a free kick against Bottom. The City goal was raided next and it was the Middlesbrough fans' turn to roar a collective 'Argh!' as Milburn of all people blasted over at point-blank range. Near the final whistle, Fenton shot tamely when in a good position, Forgan made a brave last-ditch save at Keeble's feet and Brown for City headed just wide following a last-minute corner. And after a gruelling and frustrating ninety minutes, it was still raining.

Many fans were late home that evening. Flooding in South Yorkshire made roads and railway lines impassable and there were many diversions. Still, City had lived to fight another day and had made history by becoming the first Third Division side to force a semi-final replay. Media coverage of that epic clash was muted by a national newspaper strike and City's stirring efforts went largely unreported, eyewitness accounts of the match adding to a word-of-mouth romantic saga that echoes on to this day.

The replay at Roker Park was fought out on Wednesday 30 March, a fine spring day, the mid-week tie preventing many York fans from supporting their team. Only 12,000 out of a total crowd of 58,000 saw the match, although York almost came to a standstill as supporters stood by their radios and listened to the specially relayed commentary in the Market Place. A fit Storey found his way back into the City side. Newcastle made one change, substituting Crowe for Casey at left-half.

Things went badly for the away team from the start, a third-minute goal by White from close range after a pass by Milburn stunning City. But they fought back and played the better football, although the incisive finishing that hallmarked previous rounds never came, Fenton squandering a great chance just before the break by volleying into the side netting.

City's rhythm was further upset in the first minute of the second half when Stewart collided with Keeble, sustaining a bloody gash over his left eye. He was lost to the game for twelve minutes, the team doctor patching him up with five stitches to allow him to occupy a rather ineffectual role on the wing. Effectively down to ten men, gallant City probed for an equaliser but it never came, Newcastle United executing the *coup de grâce* in the last minute when Keeble nodded home the second goal. The Wembley dream was finally extinguished, York City having some consolation in May when Newcastle beat Manchester City 3–1 to lift the FA Cup.

Just a few years later, all the heroes of that famous cup run melted away. Tommy Forgan took to laying bricks for a living; Norman Wilkinson made shoes. But all these years later still, the magic of the FA Cup lingers on, nurtured by now rare copies of the souvenir brochure, *Those Happy Wanderers* produced to honour that monumental tie at Hillsborough.

At the start of the new millennium, receiverships and massive debts apart, professional football is still thriving in its English birthplace, although resources are skewed towards teams in the Premier Division. The game in York has definitely been under threat, but the Bootham Crescent ground (now renamed Kit Kat Crescent in recognition of its confectionery sponsor) has, thanks to the sterling efforts of the supporters' trust, been saved from redevelopment, holding the prospect of a new and exciting chapter in the roller-coaster ride that has been the history of the City Reds. A secure and modernised ground . . . promotion into the Football League . . . a new FA Cup run and . . . perhaps . . . a new logo? Could we dispense with the jaded image of one of York's entrance bars and substitute something more appropriate instead? What could be more fitting than a device honouring that beautiful kick-about by Dobson and his chums in the 'cathedral church of Yorke'? The Minstermen indeed.

5

THE BAEDEKER RAID

The Second World War was vicious and brutal, and its echoes, two generations on, reverberate still. My childhood was coloured by its consequences and by the tall tales of my father, who was an able-seaman ASDIC operator aboard the aircraft carrier HMS *Implacable*. Small wonder then that my first family portrait shows a sprite wearing a sailor suit with a rather limp Union Jack in his hand. Those horrific newsreels of the Blitz and the host of post-war films glorifying in the defeat of Nazi Germany got me to waving that little flag, and I was there with the best of them in the bombed and burnt-out shell of St Hilda's School in Richmond Hill, Leeds, aiming my wooden tommy gun at the enemy. It was only years later when I began to read the more sober and horrifically accurate accounts of the multiple atrocities perpetrated by our side that I realised just how nasty we, in turn, had been to the Germans, a quirk of fate many years later still, focusing that reality even more.

Nastiness begets nastiness and in a few hours on the moonlit cusp between 28 and 29 April 1942, one such act of brutality on the German people was repaid on the City of York in full. To understand why the Luftwaffe attacked an English provincial city that boasted more churches than anti-aircraft guns and had hardly a searchlight or barrage balloon to its name, one must go back to the beginning of that fateful year and to the appointment of one of the most controversial figures of the entire war. When Arthur Harris became the head of Bomber Command on 14 February 1942, the RAF had a poor mission record over Germany. The newly dubbed 'Bomber' Harris would change all that in pursuing the prime directive of undermining the morale of the civilian population. In a chilling change of tactics that would be become known in German as 'Terrorangriff' (terror raid), he formulated a plan to bomb the largely undefended, strategically insignificant little town of Lübeck on the German coast, electing to use incendiaries in preference to high explosives. Beautiful Lübeck, a medieval city built largely of ancient timbers was, according to Harris, 'built more like a firelighter than a human habitation' and it would readily burn. 'I wanted my crews to be well-blooded, as they say in fox-hunting,' he said later. The town was the home of a U-boat training school and its docks were used for the transhipment of Swedish iron ore to German foundries but neither of these legitimate targets featured in the flight plans. On the night of Palm Sunday, 28 March 1942, 234 bombers, many from Yorkshire airfields, droned off in waves to the Baltic port, the Wellingtons and Stirlings attacking in three waves over two hours, killing 520 civilians and injuring 784 more. Operating with relative impunity from a bombing ceiling of only 2,000 feet, the aircraft destroyed nearly half the city, together with four factories, the central railway terminal and the main electricity power station, the deadly incendiaries burning the lovely thirteenth-century Marienkirche, the magnificent medieval Town Hall and hundreds of half-timbered houses. On the roof of one of them was 16-year-old Lotte Stahl, a terrified young woman who vainly tried to extinguish some of the bombs. 'People were screaming,' she recalls. 'They were climbing out of their three-storey houses, throwing their feather beds down and jumping on top. The bombers flattened Königstrasse and the surrounding area. People who hid in the cellars were suffocated alive. So many bodies; the smell hung around for years.' The conflagration took thirty-two hours to put out.

Harris lost just twelve aircraft that night – an acceptable 5 per cent – and he was joyful. Adolf Hitler was outraged and ranting, a second terror attack a month later on Rostock, prompting reprisals. The Führer was urged on by Doctor Joseph Goebbels, the Minister of Propaganda who wrote the following in his diary: 'Like the English, we must attack the centres of culture especially those which have little anti-aircraft . . . At noon I had lunch with the Führer. He is very angry at the latest attacks on Lübeck and Rostock. He shares my opinion absolutely that cultural centres, health resorts and civilian centres must be

attacked now . . . there is no other way of bringing the English to their senses. They belong to a class of human beings with whom you can only talk after you have first knocked their teeth out.'

Target selection was referred to Luftwaffe Headquarters, Chief-of-Staff General Hans Jeschonnek who knew little about England's historic cities. He turned for help to the tourist guidebook written by well-known nineteenth-century German author Karl Baedeker, noting the names of Bath, Canterbury, Exeter, Norwich and York. The list was agreed with Hitler and York's fate was sealed. For the first time since the Battle of Marston Moor in 1644, the city was endangered.

Bath and Exeter were attacked first, the raid on York following on the night of 28/29 April 1942. Although York was architecturally one of the most cherished cities in Europe, it was also an important

Damaged church in Lübeck after the RAF raid. *(Courtesy of Archiv der Hansestadt Lübeck)*

The shattered bells that dropped from the southern spire of the ancient Marienkirke after the bombing lie where they fell. *(LMA)*

railhead and rolling stock repair centre as well as a garrison town for the British Army's Northern Command. These slim realities gave the Luftwaffe a veneer of legitimacy in choosing York. The aircrews that night might have had more relish for their mission had they known that production had been suspended in part of the famous Rowntree's confectionery factory. Instead of making chocolates, the girls on the night shift now filled shell casings with high explosive.

Seventy-four aircraft – Junkers, Dorniers and Heinkels – were charged with the task of bombing three separate targets. York railway station, the subject of reconnaissance photography in October 1941, was to receive special attention. Pilots were told by an intelligence officer that if they could destroy York's signalling system, they would shut down the entire network and disrupt the distribution of vital supplies: 'and you can bet there won't be much leaving Hull for Murmansk to help the Russians for the next few weeks'.

Leutnant Mühlen piloted Do217 (U5+KP) on that cloudless night, later recalling the following in his flight log: 'We are all in good spirits and thinking of anything but the dreadful disaster that we would encounter two hours later.' Flying over the Yorkshire coast and following the silvery Ouse that would lead to the target, Mühlen and his comrades met little resistance as York slept. Only a few token bombs had previously landed on the city in 1940 and 1941, and York residents snuggled on in the conviction that 'Jerry had forgotten York'. But the flyers of Luftflotte 3 would shatter their dreams.

The blitz began at precisely 2.36 a.m. on 29 April 1942. The city was almost completely undefended but somehow, Free French Pilot Officer Yves Mahe, flying a Hurricane from his base at Hibaldstow in Lincolnshire, managed to intercept one of the attackers. But not before the rest of the aircraft had dropped their bombs.

The first wave of bombers was spectacularly successful. Poppleton Road School and St Peter's School were hit and set ablaze, and scores of houses in the Clifton and Bootham areas were smashed and burning. 'When the raid started, we all went down into the cellars,' explained St Peter's pupil Rodger Frost. 'When we came up, it looked as if the whole of York was on fire. The Minster stood out against it all.'

'I was fast asleep when the first bombs dropped,' remembered local resident Edna Blakeborough. 'It was a terrific sound. The planes were just hovering over the houses and over the buildings. There was nothing to stop them and we must have been up ten minutes before the sirens went.'

Along with her 3-year-old daughter, Edna escaped to the house next door. It received a direct hit.

'As I went round, an aircraft flew low down above me. He was so low I could see the rear gunner's face. He was in his leather, only a young man, maybe 19 or 20, and he was machine gunning me as I ran.'

'Come on now, get into the shelters,' shouted one anxious resident of Crombie Avenue. 'And remember you're British!'

'Aye', responded his neighbour, 'but do yon buggers up there know that?'

Above the prime target, the bomb doors opened and the first 250-pound device narrowly missed the newly arrived express from London. The next bomb of the stick exploded near the parcels office, dozens of incendiaries adding to the conflagration that engulfed the station roof and the track, threatening the train. Soldiers and civilians ran for their lives, Assistant Station Master Lyon and Inspector Skelton of the Railway Police leading the evacuation. Recognising the danger to the express, Lyon organised the fire fighting, enlisting the help of an unidentified soldier and shunter drivers Wharton and Lee. With parts of the burning roof falling all around, these brave men ran to their engines, pulling fourteen carriages to safety, leaving the remaining six burning fiercely on the track. Women porters all the while kicked incendiaries from the platform on to the track, Signalman Simpson leaving his damaged signal box to assist in the rescue of burning parcel vans. There was great camaraderie elsewhere, booking office staff and volunteers helping to drag burning office furniture across the road from the station for dumping in the water-filled moat at the foot of the city walls. Bombs were falling all around but two fire-watchers, who were anxious that the LNER would not lose their day's takings, snatched up the money from the booking office tills, stuffing it into a wellington

Party officials examine the devastation caused by the RAF bombing of Lübeck, Palm Sunday 1942. *(Courtesy of Archiv der Hansestadt Lübeck)*

boot and racing for the sanctuary of the Railway Hotel. Overhead, the bombers positioned themselves above the carriage works.

A high-explosive bomb immediately fell on the roundhouse. All twenty locomotives parked round the central turntable were damaged, three of them seriously. Worse affected was the crippled A4, streamlined Pacific-class engine *Sir Ralph Wedgwood*, the twisted locomotive coming to rest on its side. There was another loud explosion at the nearby Leeman Road stables, where the railway company's dray horses were kept. Ignoring the flames, Stableman Martin and two helpers leapt to the rescue, leading the nineteen horses, one by one, to safety across Martin's prize allotment. Seeing his 'Dig For Victory' garden ravaged by the mighty hooves of the Shires and Clydesdales, Martin cursed the Germans. In that moment, he was more saddened at the sight of his ruined cabbages than that of his own burning home. Onward went the bombers, dropping further sticks on the vital railway lines north of the city, although one aircraft was stuck with its load. The bomb doors refused to open on the Junkers flown by Leutnant Werner Boy and he circled hoping to make another pass. At that moment, Mahe's Hurricane approached from the rear and delivered a two-second burst that set fire to the raider's starboard engine. The Junkers crew managed to bale out from the aircraft but Boy stayed at the controls and died as the rest of the bomber force moved in over the heart of the city.

'The Rise', St Peter's School after the bombing. *(St Peter's School)*

If Lübeck had its Holstentor and Marienkirche, York had its 500-year-old Guildhall and St Martin-le-Grand church, and these were bombed next and set on fire, other high-explosive devices devastating the Post Office, the newspaper offices and the shops in the Leopard Arcade. Just 250 yards and one second's flying time to the northeast, the most prominent target of all, York Minster, remained strangely unmolested. Leaving the City Art Gallery and government offices in Duncombe Place in flames, the bombers flew along the line of Coney Street, New Street and Davygate, unleashing their pods: dozens of riverside homes, offices and warehouses took direct hits. Across the river, Rowntree's North Street depot, packed high with sugar, was burning fiercely. The casualties mounted, ambulance crews battling through the mayhem to get to the dead and dying. Some seventy-four civilians never made it. One dead mother was dragged from the rubble still clutching the lifeless body of her child in her arms. In two cases, so obliterated were the bodies that the remains had to be collected in buckets. Several nuns were killed in the Bar Convent School in tragic circumstances. Most of the sisters had fled with their pupils to the mattress-lined cellar for safety but one rather deaf and infirm sister had been left behind. Other nuns went to her rescue, five of them dying in the attempt. Three nuns were trapped in the rubble, the rest having their habits shredded in the explosion of a massive bomb. One sister's hair turned instantly white. In total that night, there were some 205 injuries.

Despite the immense danger, there were multiple acts of heroism during the raid and there were also occasional displays of black humour. One soldier emerged from a cellar cocking a service revolver with the words: 'They say Jerry drops parachutists during the cover of a raid and I'm going out to shoot them.'

'Put that gun away!' shouted his landlady. 'The way I feel at the moment – if any German parachutist lands here, I'll strangle him personally with my own bare hands.'

Their mission accomplished, the bombers headed for home, Leutnant Mühlen in his Dornier Do217 (U5+KP) recording the following in his flight log: 'The bombs have gone and with them the prickly feeling of tension. Nothing else can happen to us – or so we think. Out thoughts are once again on the beauty and pleasantness of our home base in Soesterberg.' Then a night fighter (it was probably a Beaufighter from Scorton, although the official accounts are ambiguous) swoops out of darkness and lets fly with several bursts of machine-gun fire and the Dornier is hit and crippled, eventually crash-landing at Coneysthorpe near Malton. One man, the Dornier's wireless operator, died but Mühlen and the rest of his crew survived and were taken prisoner. In addition to Boy's Junkers, only two other aircraft were lost in the entire attack, Jeschonnek matching Harris's 5 per cent with a creditable 5 per cent of his own. Over fifty years on, Dr Karl-Heinz Mühlen, who remained a prisoner of war until 1945, said this about his actions: 'What did I feel when I was dropping the bombs? I knew that women and children would die, but we were soldiers, we didn't think about that. It wasn't until I was in the prison camp that I began to realise what I had done with my bombs – how I had killed people whom I didn't know, and whom I had nothing against.'

Codeword 'PURPLE' at 2.36 a.m. ushered in the worst attack on York in three centuries; codeword 'WHITE' at 4.46 a.m. brought the emergency to a close. With the dawn came the awful reality of two hours of carnage that had resulted in the destruction of or damage to 9,500 houses and hundreds of warehouses, businesses and shops. Parts of the great city lay in ruins. Its railway station had been put out of action and some of its ancient treasures including the irreplaceable fifteenth-century stained glass in St Martin's Church had gone for ever. It was a morning for quiet reflection and for cleaning up, shopkeepers sweeping myriad shards of glass into neat piles outside their premises, housewives setting to with mops, buckets and dusters, and postmen completing their rounds with cheery tunes on their lips as if nothing had happened. BUSINESS AS USUAL, read one defiant sign. BOMBED BUT NOT BEATEN read another, the stoical character of York residents figuring in the sensational news reports of one journalist who reported on 'people laughing and talking about their experiences. They might have been a holiday crowd walking out in the sunshine. I have seen people looking less happy

The smouldering ruins of
St Martin's Church in Coney
Street, York, after the air raid.
(York & County Press)

at Blackpool.' Inevitably, many people with a morbid interest in the death and destruction flocked to the city and signs had to be displayed on entrance routes proclaiming NO SIGHTSEERS, the police turning away the cars of drivers who had no legitimate reason for visiting York. The day after the raid, a formal meeting was held to assess how the authorities had coped. The official verdict amid the self-congratulation and the jingoistic exhortations of the press was one of quiet satisfaction, but beneath the roar of approval was a murmur: 'Where was the bloody RAF?' After the memorial service that was held in the undamaged Minster a week later, that burning question was on everyone's lips.

Adolf Hitler had an eye-for-an-eye mentality that was utterly predictable. So why, after such a devastating attack on Lübeck, was a retaliatory strike against York not anticipated, especially after earlier, similar raids on the comparable picture-postcard towns of Bath and Exeter? Harold Nicolson MP had certainly voiced his own fears and the thorn-in-the-side peace activist Vera Brittain had constantly raised her concerns. The lack of any sort of defence short of fortuitous interceptions by a small number of fighter aircraft, was strange indeed, until one realises, that York might perhaps have been expendable in favour of the greater strategic good.

Operation Ultra was one of the most important and closely guarded secrets of the Second World War. Based initially on work by Polish intelligence officers, refined, adapted and vastly expanded by staff at Bletchley Park in Buckinghamshire under the direction of Alan Turing, Ultra was devoted to cracking German codes. Transmitted by highly sophisticated Enigma coding machines, top-secret orders were thought to be decipher-immune (the odds against such an unlikely eventuality were 150 million, million, million to 1) until Turing and his staff of mathematicians, cryptographers and crossword-puzzle experts, assisted by a genius telecommunications engineer called Tommy Flowers, built the world's first programmable, electronic computer called Colossus. This enabled even the most sophisticated German codes to be broken, including the Lorenz Cipher used by the Nazi High Command. From then on, the Allies were always one jump ahead although an anticipatory jump too soon might have prejudiced the entire operation. Were encoded messages about the raid on York intercepted and passed on to the Luftwaffe cipher specialists in Hut 6 at Bletchley Park? Were these decoded and given to the RAF? And was dispensable York left to burn?

In May 1942, the Dean of York spoke of the desire to erect a monument to the dead of York. It was never built. In the same month, during a General Synod speech, the Archbishop of Canterbury protested at the destruction of Lübeck and Rostock. His complaints were brushed aside as the first of the 1,000 bomber raids on the heart of Germany began.

In 1986, the official photographs of the destruction of York were finally released by the censor, allowing the public to see the extent of the damage inflicted in 1942 for the first time. Over sixty years on, York is now twinned with the German town of Munster and Coventry is culturally linked with Lübeck in a spirit of reconciliation. Both York and Lübeck have been painstakingly restored to their former glories and that young German girl, who fought so hard to save her house at 85 Königstrasse, became my mother-in-law.

Plaques beside the entrance to the Freemason's Lodge on Schildstrasse, Lübeck. *(LMA)*

Johannis-Loge
Zum Füllhorn
- 1772 -

Johannis-Loge
Zur Weltkugel
- 1779 -

Kapitel   Konzil
York Ritus
- 1993 -

In 2006, my wife and I visited Lübeck for the first time together. It was an emotional trip. We spent a morning in the Archiv der Hansestadt Lübeck taking photographs and examining the official German records of the RAF raid, numerous outraged letters from senior party officials and one still chilling and menacing list of Jewish residents marked for attention. Afterwards, with our cameras, we made a tour of the restored churches whose burning spires had done so much to define the senseless barbarity of the attack. And soberly, arm in arm with tears in our eyes, we walked along the punctuated line of Königstrasse, the newer, more modern buildings interspersed between the ancient, high and ornate Dutch-gabled houses that survived the destruction, graphically showing where the bombs fell. We came to Lotte's old house and entered what is now a clothing shop, remembering her father Hermann Stahl, a prominent local businessman and freemason who, we understand from the testimony of surviving Jews, put his life on the line by organising escape routes. Amazingly, we discovered yet further associations with York. On the corner of Schildstrasse is Hermann's still surviving lodge house, a brass plaque at its entrance proclaiming an affiliation with its counterpart in York. A few streets away in Mengstrasse is a building with even more significance. It is called Buddenbrooks after Thomas Mann's 1929 Nobel Prize-winning novel of the same name. Apart from the façade, it was completely destroyed by the bombing but it has now been painstakingly rebuilt and dedicated as a museum to the talented Mann family who once lived in the town, the irrepressible Erika Mann who once famously lampooned the Nazi regime in her 1933 cabaret *Pepper Mill*, marrying York poet W.H. Auden in 1932. The dismembered family had to flee Hitler's tyranny and Thomas and his brother Heinrich found sanctuary in the United States. On hearing about the RAF raid and the destruction of his childhood home in 1942, Thomas remarked: 'The old residence which they say now lies in rubble was for me a symbol of the tradition from which I worked. But such rubble doesn't scare one who lives not only out of sympathy for the past, but also for the future.'

Opposite: Workers scour the ruins of the Bar Convent where five nuns were killed. *(City of York Council www.imagineyork.co.uk)*

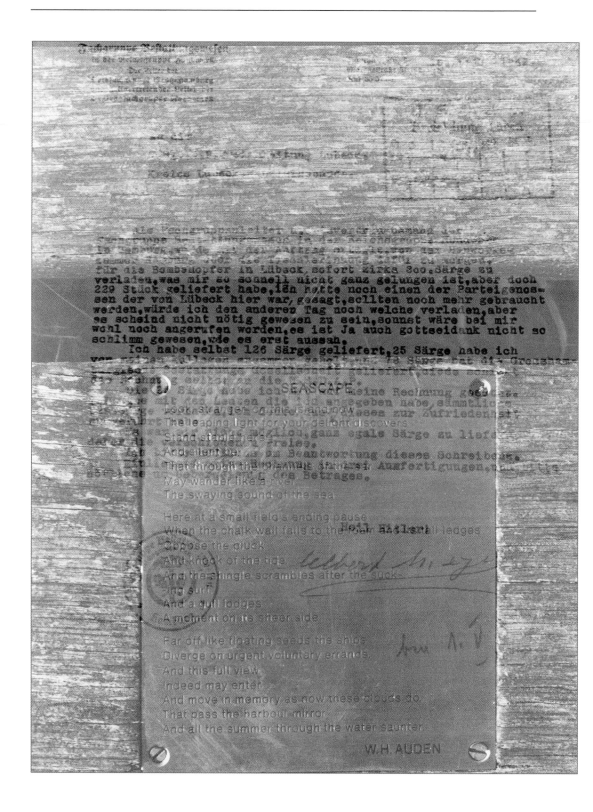

SEASCAPE

Look, stranger, on this island now
The leaping light for your delight discovers,
Stand stable here
And silent be,
That through the channels of the ear
May wander like a river
The swaying sound of the sea

Here at a small field's ending pause
When the chalk wall falls to the foam and its tall ledges
Oppose the pluck
And knock of the tide,
And the shingle scrambles after the suck-
ing surf,
And a gull lodges
A moment on its sheer side.

Far off like floating seeds the ships
Diverge on urgent voluntary errands,
And this full view
Indeed may enter
And move in memory as now these clouds do,
That pass the harbour mirror
And all the summer through the water saunter.

W.H. AUDEN

The restored Buddenbrooks House in Lübeck, former home of the Mann family. *(LMA)*

POSTSCRIPT

A week after we arrived back from Lübeck, my film was returned from the processors. I opened the envelope and stared at four of the photographs in annoyance and some amazement. They were all double exposed. 'But they can't be! My old but thoroughly reliable Pentax ME Super – it's not failed me once in two decades – won't allow this.' I checked the camera. It was working perfectly . . . no fault there. And then I studied the photographs and gasped. The underlying images are of my wife in summer clothes and of a poetic tribute on a bench, to a deceased couple, Toby and Grace, set high above our home in Eastbourne on the downs overlooking the sea. The tribute is on an affixed plaque, the engraved words reproducing the poem *Seascape* by W.H. Auden. On my photograph, the image of the plaque is overlain with one of a memorandum sent from Fachgruppe Bestattungswessen in Hamburg to an official in Lübeck on 16 April 1942. The photograph is shown opposite.

6

THE ETON OF THE
NORTH

Founded in AD 627, St Peter's School, York, is older than most countries and has lasted longer than some empires. According to some, it may not be quite the oldest still-surviving educational establishment in England, but it is not far short. A force for enlightenment in one of the greatest cathedral cities of Europe, it stands alongside its ecclesiastical namesake as a proud beacon of York in the new millennium, its continuing reputation for academic excellence spanning the globe.

St Peter's was co-founded with the Minster by Paulinus as a grammar and song school, converts to the religion of Rome requiring knowledge of the church vernacular to enable them to participate in liturgy and church services. Nurtured by successive archbishops of York, it developed as a grammar school for the rich and wealthy from England and abroad, its curriculum embracing grammar, rhetoric (the art of correct expression and argument), law, poetry, music, astronomy, natural history, geometry, the ecclesiastical calendar and divinity. Under the tutelage of Archbishop Albert and Alcuin, a former pupil who became master of Charlemagne's Palace School and one of the finest academics of his age, St Peter's prospered on a site near the Minster, becoming famed as the best school north of the Alps. And it built up one of the most comprehensive libraries in Europe, the priceless collection of books surviving the anarchy of the late Saxon period and the depredations of the Danes. Three years after the Norman Conquest, however, in an act of vandalism probably only surpassed in history by the destruction of the book repository in the ancient city of Alexandria, the library was destroyed along with the school, restoration eventually taking place on a new site, probably south of the Minster.

During the medieval period, St Peter's had three integrated faculties consisting of a song school, a theological school and a grammar school. Places were almost exclusively reserved for children of the nobility or for the offspring of entrepreneurs who made fortunes in business and trade, but even in this educationally unenlightened period, some poorer students were encouraged with bursaries. At the time of the Reformation, the religious ethos that had influenced every facet of life at St Peter's underwent a major review. Its constitution was amended and updated to reflect the new radicalism, the loss of financial support for fifty boarders, who had been maintained by stipends given by the abbot of St Mary's in York, causing the proprietors of the school to move to new premises in the Hospital of St Mary in Horsefair. Endowed with generous grants, the new establishment became known as the Free Grammar School, providing education and board and lodging for fifty boys, the inspirational headmaster John Pullen creating a centre of learning that was widely regarded as one of the best in the country.

Before 1557, the administration of the school was the responsibility of the Chancellor. After that date, control was vested in the Dean and Chapter in pursuit of Cardinal Pole's mission to 'convert the stiff-necked citizens of York to Catholicism'.

By 1557, the school was run under a Royal Charter, occupying premises in a former hospital in the Horsefair just outside the city walls. These premises were destroyed during the Civil War, and the school relocated to a building known as the Bedern, whose original use was as a refectory and dormitory for Minster clergy. The school remained in the Bedern for eighty-six years, until it was rehoused briefly in the Bagnio – once a Turkish bathhouse – pupils leaving there in 1735 for the disused church of St Andrew's in St Andrewgate. For nearly a century, St Peter's operated from this rather unsuitable building, its standards of teaching and its reputation declining over the years. After a thankfully brief interlude occupying what had been Mr Noke's Dancing Academy, the school moved to a new building – The Minster School – in the Minster Yard in 1833. Then in 1844 came a dramatic change in fortune. A prominent York architect called John Harper had been commissioned by a group of prominent businessmen to design a new purpose-built proprietary school. He produced an ornate building that was architecturally superior to anything the city had seen before. Harper built his school in a revival Perpendicular Gothic style in 1838, choosing a site in the salubrious environs of Clifton upstream from the bustle of York. The school cost £3,200 to erect. The Revd William Hey was appointed as Principal at an annual salary of £500. Tuition fees were set at £10 per year and board at 30 guineas. Boys were taken from 6 years old. School hours were from 9 a.m. to 12 noon and 2 p.m. to 5 p.m., Monday to Friday. Saturday was a half holiday. The school was closed for six weeks' holiday in midsummer and for four weeks at Christmas. By 1844, this proprietary school had amalgamated with the Minster School, the combined complement of pupils totalling 101 boys. Considerably enlarged and embellished, St Peter's has remained at Clifton ever since, students becoming collectively known as 'Peterites', the combined complement of students of all ages now totalling almost 1,000.

For twenty years, the new school flourished under the guidance of Hey, who won the heart of every boy. He was described as a humble and generous man with a sunny disposition and an innate sense of fairness and justice. But boys will be boys, and even the tolerant Hey and his housemasters had to set strict rules. School boundaries were rigorously defined and a system of fines imposed for infringements. Boys who trespassed on to the grass plot in front of the school were fined 6d. Boys who visited the tuck shop outside the prescribed times were fined 1s and no boy was allowed to smoke or to have in his possession gunpowder

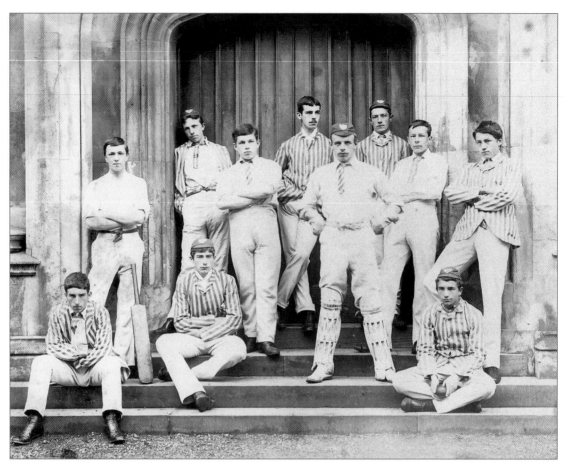

St Peter's School cricket 1st XI, *c*. 1888. *(St Peter's School)*

or firearms. The payment of fines did not end there. Many boys were fond of playing football in the playground. Occasionally, the ball would become lodged on top of the projecting oriel window that was a feature of the Big Hall. The cost for retrieval by the school carpenter was 1*s*. The rigid regimes at schools such St Peter's developed some highly individual scholars and some eccentric masters who were parodied in later times by writers such as Frank Richards who wrote so humorously about Billy Bunter and Mr Quelch – the scourge of every boy with a penchant for cream buns. One such character who stalked the Clifton corridors of the 1850s was the Revd W.J. Thompson. A stern and imposing figure who persistently flashed his cane like a cattle prod, he was known to his charges in the Fourth Form as 'Old Bull' or 'Darky Thompson'. His colleague, M. Habersak, was nicknamed 'The Smasher', both these men subscribing to the traditional notion that education should be based on the three Bs – the boy, the book and the birch. Both martinets might have stolen the thunder of other imposing masters, but one man, the legendary Revd Thomas Richardson, boomed louder still. Squat and bow-legged with a waddling gait, a broad Yorkshire accent and an acerbic wit, he had a most singular method of teaching, using what became known as 'Tommy Cards'. Measuring 5 inches by 3 inches, these cards were impressed with names and dates, pupils having to recite the details from memory or face the wrath of old 'Tommy'. On one side of the cards were religious subjects such as the lists and the chronology of the kings of Judah. On the other were astronomical and historical topics such as the names of the twelve signs of the zodiac and the monarchs of England. The threat of a close encounter with 'Doctor Cure 'Em Quick' persuaded each boy to learn the facts by rote, some fellows readily recalling the mantra sixty years later! In class, Richardson would suddenly shout out: 'Now my lads – which shall we have – a sum or verses?' The pupils would decide and a question would be posed, the first boy scribbling down his answer on a slate and rushing to the front in a spirit of competition. Each boy would do this in turn, taking his place in the front rows, the dullards and dunces having to occupy the seats in the rear. Sometimes Richardson would taunt his pupils, saying: 'You've not done well this morning lads, we'd better come this afternoon. And isn't it a fine afternoon?' At other times he would perk up the classroom mood, promising: 'Well my lads, I'm going to leave you.' When all the boys were happily grinning, he would knock the smiles from their faces adding: 'But when am I leaving? Not so long as I can be of any use to this institution.'

During that period, the values and vicissitudes of the public school system had been drawn to the attention of a fascinated public by Thomas Hughes's famous book *Tom Brown's Schooldays*, published in 1857. It centred on the life of the eponymous pupil during the period of his education at Rugby School in the 1830s, but many of the privations the young lad endured at that establishment equally applied to the quadrangles at York. St Peter's had its own senior boys, Yorkshire equivalents of Flashman, who delighted in the oppression of younger pupils. Fagging was a common feature of school life at St Peter's until comparatively recent times, former pupil Rodger Frost relating his experiences to me as a newly arrived 14-year-old boy in 1938. Fagging was the sanctioned drudgery of younger boys, who were expected to perform menial and often demeaning tasks without any recompense for house monitors and prefects. Before breakfast, new entrants were called upon to tidy up studies, to organise books and documents and to clean and polish such things as football and rugby boots. They were also required to uproot plantains from the football pitch, some of the more savvy types selling their weeds to fellow fags. Veritable slaves, fags could be called upon at any time for a whole year, and Flashman types, who were dissatisfied with the work done, had the right to chastise the fag with a slipper. 'Some of the monitors took huge delight at beating a fag,' explained Mr Frost. 'The masters used to cane us on the backside with a stick but the monitors were only allowed to use a slipper. But they always inflicted the maximum pain by using the heel end. They could give you a maximum of six strokes. You had the right of appeal to a housemaster but nobody ever wanted to be thought of as a squealer. And do you know what time we went to bed? It was 9 o'clock even in summer. And we had a ghost!'

St Peter's School pageant group, 1909.
(St Peter's School)

Tommy Richardson who was adept with the use of the cane served St Peter's for forty-four years. While he was in his prime, the school was enlarged and in 1856 a Civil and Military Department was inaugurated, the comprehensive school curriculum being further extended with the inclusion of new subjects embracing surveying, fortification and maritime navigation. In 1860 the St Peter's Cadet Corps was established by a militaristic assistant master – the son of a general. Fifty boys volunteered to join, height determining who would receive a rifle or a sword. The little boys found their weapons were ideal for toasting muffins!

By 1864, the school had expanded again to cater for 150 boys, 90 of whom were boarders. By 1875, the school had added more science subjects to the curriculum. In 1878, the Debating Society was established and the first edition of the school magazine – the *Peterite* – was published. A year later, sixth-form students were first examined by the Oxford and Cambridge Schools' Examination Board. Not only did matriculating students gain entry into the portals of two of the finest universities in the world, but they also made it into the hallowed ranks of the oarsmen who yearly contested the famous boat race on the Thames. Regular practice on the Ouse – the 'sooty Ouse' in the Song of the St Peter's Rowers of 1936 – was encouraged by some rather vociferous masters who were experts both in the use of the cane and the megaphone.

> The waters of the Ouse
> Are troubled by the storm;
> The tempests lash the crews
> And leave them far from warm.
> Do the icy tempests pause?
> Do the oarsmen ask them why?
> So we row without a cause
> 'Neath the bleak, grey sky.

Uniquely, Old Peterite G.L. Davis was cox of the Cambridge University boat for five consecutive years and was involved in the dead-heat race of 1877.

Following reorganisation of the Governing Body in 1898, a new, more modern constitution was drafted, although the school still maintained links with the Dean and Chapter and the Archbishop of York. At the beginning of the new century, the school entered into a phase of further expansion and development, playing its part in the national struggle during the years of the Great War, when the St Peter's Corps was reorganised and extended. The boys also supported the School Base Hospital in Boulogne and, in the absence of hundreds of able-bodied men who were fighting in Flanders, they performed all sorts of mundane but vital tasks such as the conversion of the school playing fields for vegetable cultivation. On three occasions during 1916, German Zeppelins darkened the York skies, one airship droning over the school as the boys slept. Woken by up by gunfire, they were ushered into the cellars for safety, searchlights illuminating the attacker just north of the school. Bursting with a mixture of dread and excitement, the boys looked out to witness a direct hit on the undercarriage of one Zeppelin, a large contingent rushing out in their night attire to cheer the gunners on. One chap was injured by a piece of shrapnel but the school was unharmed. During a similar but more sustained attack by the German air force in the early hours of 29 April 1942, the school was not so lucky. Fortunately, most boys were holidaying at the time and the dormitories were almost empty. High-explosive bombs damaged the rugby pitch, ripped off large sections of roof tiles and shattered nearly every pane of glass in the entire school. Incendiaries caused the greatest damage, though, fires gutting the 'Long' and 'Incubator' dormitories of School House and destroying the front portion of Clifton Rise. That morning, the BBC broke the news to a shocked nation that York had been bombed and its famous school obliterated. The bulletins were amended during the day and by the time the new term started just a few frantic days later, the school had been patched up and makeshift accommodation provided.

Since 1945, the school has been enlarged and thoroughly modernised to cater for the demands of the twenty-first century, the current co-educational boarding school providing facilities for children from the ages of 4 to 18.

In such a short chapter as this, it is impossible to do justice to an institution that has existed for nearly 1,400 years. Several books could be devoted to the work of successive headmasters, and accounts of the lives of former pupils who made their marks on the world might fill a whole library. St Peter's has been led by many men of accomplishment such as Alcuin and St John of Beverley, some of the lesser acolytes who served the school with great devotion and distinction being remembered in the names of the school halls. A visit to the ancient precincts wafts up other names from the hall of fame, a tour of an old garden discovering the intertwined names of a former master George Yeld and clumps of fragrant *hemerocallis*, the fabled Day Lily. Yeld lived in the nearby cottage and spent many leisure hours on the pioneering propagation of his favourite flower, enthusiasts still arriving at St Peter's on the trail of his original 'Apricot' coloured Day Lily, that was first hybridised in 1892. Over 40,000 registered varieties are now available. Near Yeld's cottage garden, the lists of famous ex-pupils are proudly displayed in refectories and halls, the names including those of Rear Admiral N.F. Roy, Air Chief Marshal Sir Charles Medhurst, Professor S.N. Parkinson, the originator of 'Parkinson's Law', P. St G. Kirke, engineer, author and inventor, poet laureate Laurence Eusden, John Barry the composer, England cricket-team captain Norman Yardley and one man who is remembered in flame every year.

In the sixteenth century, John Pullen created a school that was envied for its academic achievements, but there is some intrigue surrounding his religious leanings. An influential man, he latterly presided over St Peter's at a time when rumours of Papist plots were rife and it is fascinating to discover that four out of the thirteen men who conspired to eliminate Parliament in 1605 were his pupils. Guy Fawkes, who was born in York in 1570, was one of them. His classmate accomplices were Oswald Tessimond and brothers John and Christopher Wright. St Peter's historians claim one other name for the blacklist, that of Edward Oldcorne. Every schoolboy knows the story of the fuse-burner's fateful discovery in the Parliament cellars and his subsequent execution. And every schoolboy, apart from those who have attended St Peter's since 1937, has celebrated the burning of his effigy every year on the eve of 5 November. In 1937 – before that date the suffragette Mrs Pankhurst got a good toasting – the headmaster decreed that effigies of old boys should not be burnt. That edict has been honoured ever since.

Like the twentieth century's Nelson Mandela and his own brand of freedom fighters, Guy Fawkes and his fellow conspirators were idealists, and, in writing the conclusion to this chapter, I cannot help but reflect on the eternal nature of idealism. In the 1,400 years since Paulinus first founded St Peter's, devils and dynasties have come and gone, and yet his creation grows benignly on by the waters of the now not-so-sooty Ouse. And what of the reverberating claim that St Peter's is the oldest school in the land? Well, according to the school archivist, the matter was settled long ago. In 1937, at the time of the school's 1,300 anniversary, a rugby match was played against the other contender for the longevity crown to finally decide the matter. St Peter's thrashed King's School, Canterbury, 13–9. QED.

7
'FRESH AND DAINTY'

In the art of preparing food, the French are supreme, their chefs magically transforming even humble ingredients into dishes fit for the gods. Look in any continental patisserie window and drool over the pastries and cakes, the combination of transmuted flours, sugars, colourful fruit and cream catching the eye like rare jewels. The displays in our own bakeries are traditionally dull in comparison. What gourmet can get excited at the sight of coconut macaroons, custard slices and apple turnovers? You may search the entire nation for something to impassion the lips but if by some miracle you find yourself in Yorkshire and are attracted moth-like to certain emporium windows in Harrogate, Ilkley, Northallerton and York, your quest will be over. If the French cockerel is represented by the éclair, we have an equally toothsome bulldog in the shape of the fat rascal created by Betty's, one of the most famous brand names in England.

I have to admit that although Betty's is the very essence of Englishness, redolent of Noel Coward, afternoon tea and Crown Derby, it was established by a foreigner – a Swiss national named Frederick Belmont. Frederick came from the tiny hamlet of Leiman near Berne, where his father was the village miller and baker. The father was tragically killed in a bakehouse fire, leaving Frederick's mother with little means of support for her young family. She had no option but to send Frederick out to work. He was fostered out to a farmer in a neighbouring parish and spent most of his teenage years as a labourer. But he had a dream of emulating his father and he worked hard, eventually saving enough money to fund his ambitions. At the turn of the last century, he set out for Paris to train as a confectioner. After a few years, he became an expert with the piping nozzle and in 1907, buoyed by the success of other Swiss compatriots such as César Ritz, who had opened a new hotel in London, he decided to head for England to open his own business. His original intention was to settle in either of the fashionable seaside resorts of Eastbourne or Bournemouth. So why did he finish up in Harrogate? Because his English was non-existent and when he arrived in London, seeking out Victoria, he found himself completely disoriented in King's Cross instead. Frederick had no money to buy a ticket back to London, but the beautiful Yorkshire countryside and its sweet alpine-like air reminded him of his native Switzerland. So he decided to stay, and by the end of the First World War, having married a local girl named Claire, he was ready to realise his dreams. After the gloom of the conflict, Harrogate was poised to resume its role as one of the premier spa towns in Europe and Frederick caught the mood in 1919, opening his first café just a few yards from the door of the Royal Baths. The enterprise was an instant hit. How could it be otherwise when aristocratic lords and ladies, crown princes and princesses from several European courts and well-heeled business people clamoured for antidotes to the foul-tasting chalybeate and sulphur waters? Frederick regaled them in some style, producing everything 'fresh and dainty' and before long his notepaper bore the legend: 'Under Royal and Distinguished Patronage', the constant stream of affluent customers allowing him to charge premium prices and to plan for bigger things.

With a comfortable income, the Belmonts had an opportunity to enjoy the holiday experience of a lifetime in 1936. On 27 May, they joined 2,000 other elite passengers on board the prestigious Cunard liner *Queen Mary* as she sailed on her maiden voyage to New York. Food might have been Frederick's preoccupation on the three weeks' voyage, but it was the ship's ambience and décor that caught his attention most. He was totally captivated by the designer's sumptuous use of tropical timbers, classical architecture and works of art in creating the most magnificent ship afloat, and he was particularly inspired by the inlaid marquetry of a man named Charles Spindler. Gazing and scribbling notes, Frederick spent most of the voyage planning his own tour de force and, by the time the ship docked, he had decided to open a second café in his favourite Yorkshire city of York.

By now, the naturalised Yorkshireman had developed a nose for business. The modern estate agents' mantra about the importance of location had not yet been coined but Frederick was fifty years ahead of his time and chose his site well. He selected a dilapidated furniture store on the corner of St Helen's Square at the bottom of Stonegate as the base for his new flagship café and, armed with the scribbles made aboard the *Queen Mary*, he brought in the craftsmen.

No expense was spared in recreating the sumptuous salon atmosphere of the big ship. The old furniture store was stripped bare and specialist shop fitters were brought up from London to install the finest timber panelling, pillars and intricate mouldings. Pride of place was given to a commissioned piece of marquetry by Charles and Paul Spindler, whose workshop was traced to the tiny Alsatian village of St Leonard in eastern France. The pair replicated their lakeside and wildfowl scene made originally for the liner and it was fitted in the first-floor Belmont Room. On the ground floor was the enticing café and shop selling mouth-watering breads, cakes and pastries. The Oak Room occupied the basement and on the top floor was the Ballroom, dazzlingly accoutred with crystal chandeliers, softly lit ceiling domes and gold satin curtains. With exquisite timing, York's newest attraction was scheduled to open a year to the day since Frederick had disembarked in New York. The city was *en fête* for the celebrations on 1 June 1937. Hundreds of people gathered in St Helen's Square to watch the grand opening ceremony attended by the Lord Mayor and other civic dignitaries, and afterwards there was a lavish champagne reception in the Ballroom.

From the outset, Frederick offered his customers a refined dining experience that few competitors could match. All his dough was initially kneaded by hand in wooden troughs and he baked his breads in a wood-fired oven. Every other delicacy was lovingly made by hand with great expertise using only the finest and

Early advertisement for Taylor's Cafés. Taylor's joined the Betty empire in 1962. *(Published in Waddington's Yorkshire Almanack in 1924)*

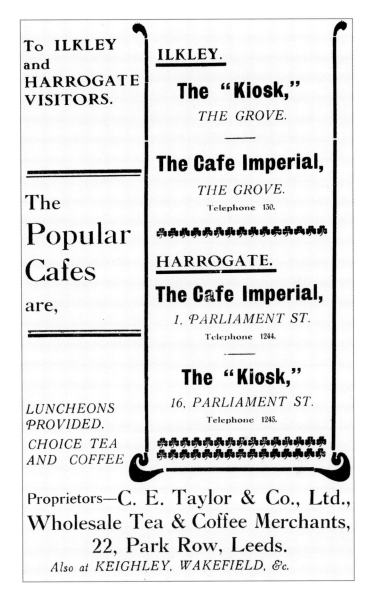

To ILKLEY and HARROGATE VISITORS.

ILKLEY.

The "Kiosk,"

THE GROVE.

The Cafe Imperial,

THE GROVE.

Telephone 130.

HARROGATE.

The Cafe Imperial,

1, PARLIAMENT ST.

Telephone 1244.

The "Kiosk,"

16, PARLIAMENT ST.

Telephone 1245.

The

Popular

Cafes

are,

LUNCHEONS PROVIDED.
CHOICE TEA AND COFFEE

Proprietors—C. E. Taylor & Co., Ltd., Wholesale Tea & Coffee Merchants, 22, Park Row, Leeds.
Also at KEIGHLEY, WAKEFIELD, &c.

freshest of ingredients. And what confidence and nerve he had! Frederick dared to sell handcrafted truffles, pralines and Easter eggs under the very noses of two of the foremost chocolate manufacturers in the county. Rowntree's and Terry's were not amused.

'Rendezvous' at Betty's became synonymous with elegance and style, the 'mountains of golden loaves, buns, scones, muffins and cakes spilling their heavenly scents like an invisible river through the door and on to the pavement', where penniless youngsters, with their noses pressed to the window and fingers pointing to some particular cake, reserved their fancies with cries of 'Bags that!' At a time of great competition from rival cafés, people returned time after time to St Helen's Square, often paying a few shillings more for the unique Betty's experience. 'A visit to Betty's nourishes your Englishness' said one regular diner, 'so that when you step outside after your cream tea, all the hard, sharp edges are blunted and muted for a while, replaced by a sense of harmony, of elegance, of civility, of mellow richness, of old English virtues that you thought had gone for ever.' That Englishness was what kept the emporium going during the Second World War.

Acting on the intuitive business acumen that had become such a hallmark of his career, Frederick applied for a liquor licence just before war was declared. It was an inspired decision. Within a few months, hundreds of allied airmen flocked to his new Betty's Bar nicknamed the 'Dive' and the 'Briefing Room' by RAF and Canadian Air Force crews. 'Fresh and dainty' gave way to 'dried and ersatz', while fish cakes, Spam fritters and corned beef hash replaced the more genteel sweetmeats of the 1930s. There was plenty of beer, of course, and no shortage of bonhomie and raucous laughter, levity and humour masking the pre-ops nerves of hundreds of flyers, many of whom never returned. The names of some of the men who never came back are etched on a poignant reminder of the war years that still survives in the modern Betty's basement. The Betty's mirror, although it was damaged in an air raid, still bears over 600 servicemen's scratched signatures. Typical examples include 'Lt.Robert Mattison US Army', 'Butsy Butson, Toronto', 'J Taylor HMS Rodney (sunk)', 'F.B. Leach', 'Sunco' Leeds', 'RAF Concert Party Broadcast Aero Follies 5/11/41', 'A.R. Turner alleged comic' and 'James W. Keilly shot down 22/5/44'. And there is one woman's moniker among the rest – 'Yvonne Skaife Betty's shop June 10 1943'. There are two theories as to how the autographing came about. One suggests it was encouraged by Frederick after he saw celebrities signing a mirror aboard the *Queen Mary*. Another supposes that it was a spontaneous affair originated by a pilot who wanted to leave a personal memento behind. He is said to have started the trend by scratching his signature with a waitress's diamond ring.

Betty's soon became a national institution, but it might have been very different had the War Office prevailed with its attempts to requisition the site for use as an administrative centre. Its clientele were outraged and many of the regulars, including several senior officers from Bomber Command, managed to thwart the proposals.

By 1944, the café was well known even to the Germans, a cartoon in the November edition of *Tatler* magazine showing a sober-looking group of military men tactically examining a map. One general points to the centre of operations with a stick, uttering the words: 'Here's Betty's Bar.'

After the war, Betty's reverted seamlessly to its traditional role, the lifting of rationing enabling it to offer luxury dishes and foods in each of its stores. The founder of the company died in 1952 but his relatives took over, and the old man's influence lives on. The number of lines was significantly increased and then, in 1962, the empire was significantly expanded with the acquisition of the Taylor family business. Like Betty's, Taylor's of Harrogate ran tea-shops but they also

Who could resist the lure of a hot crumpet on a dark and perishingly cold winter's afternoon? A view of Betty's in York with the Mansion House in the background. *(Bettys & Taylors of Harrogate)*

specialised in the provision of tea and coffee, and they had a small importing and roasting operation. The purchase complemented Betty's core business that now employs scores of staff in six locations. A recent offshoot of the company's continuing success has been the launch of a cookery school in Harrogate. True to Frederick Belmont's original ideals, it teaches the secrets of continental bread-making and the art of cooking Swiss specialities. All five Yorkshire cafes, including Little Betty's in York's Stonegate, continue to do well, regular queues telling their own story.

Betty's fulfils timeless customer needs but it does much more. An innovative company that subscribes to the modern concept of corporate social responsibility, the family business is aware of its impact on the world, developing long-term relationships with its tea and coffee growers who are guaranteed fair returns for their crops regardless of fluctuations in world commodity prices. The company has recently set up a 5 per cent fund, in which that amount of post-tax profits go to good works both in the UK and overseas. And in 1990 an environmental

A mouth-watering display of Betty's cakes. *(Bettys & Taylors of Harrogate)*

initiative was launched to plant a million trees across the world. By 2006, an impressive three million trees had actually been planted in places such as India, Ethiopia, Nicaragua and Guatemala, customers contributing to the company's Trees for Life appeal by collecting special savings tokens on packs of tea and coffee. Nearer home Betty's has worked with a charity called the Yorkshire Dales Millennium Trust, part of the profits from the sale of tree-shaped biscuits going to a re-afforestation scheme in the Dales; local retailers qualify for a tree planting for every carton of Yorkshire Tea sold.

Since Frederick bought his run-down furniture store in 1919, Betty's has been an essential part of the York experience and, along with a visit to the nearby Minster, has been included in the itineraries of every visitor and tourist. They sit in the window seats eating their Yorkshire curd tarts and imperiously watch the world go by, raising their china cups to toast Betty. But just who was this Betty? There are a number of theories.

The homely and lovable name Betty may honour a little girl who died of tuberculosis at the time her father's medical practice in Harrogate was converted into Frederick's first café. It may also be a tribute to the late Queen Mother – Elizabeth Bowes Lyon. Betty Lupton, a lady known as the 'Queen of the Harrogate Wells', is another candidate, although some people claim that a popular musical show of the time was the inspiration. The most likely explanation, however, alludes to a child called Betty Rose. This cherubic member of the Belmont family may have toddled into a board meeting during a discussion to decide on a new name for the company . . . and *voilà*! One of the descendants of great-uncle Frederick who is currently at the helm is reticent on the subject. 'The identity of the original "Betty" is a family secret,' admits company chairman Jonathan Wild. 'It's a mystery which we are determined should remain unsolved . . . eat your fat rascal, Mr Markham!'

8

AND THEY'RE OFF!

If horse racing is the sport of kings, thousands of Yorkshiremen have royal blood in their veins, the best of the seasonal transfusions in the north of England taking place at York's famous Knavesmire. A green and pleasant sward on the south side of the city centre bounded by modern housing, the River Ouse and the A64 bypass, it miraculously survives into the twenty-first century like Harrogate's Stray, its hundreds of unmolested acres and the very latest in facilities for discerning punters providing a regal setting for some of the best flat racing in Europe.

The rascally sounding Knavesmire seems tailor-made for its association with the outlaw Dick Turpin, who was executed there in 1739. The name, however, derives prosaically from the Anglo-Saxon word 'knab', meaning a serf or servant. Poor subsistence farmers of the time were readily identified with the flood-prone grazing land that would one day form the racecourse.

The Romans began the long tradition of racing in York. A casual and spontaneous activity between individuals and army units, it survived into medieval times and was revived by the turf-mad Henry VIII who created a fashion for all things equestrian. In 1530, the Lord Mayor of York donated a precious bell for annual competition between riders on nearby Clifton Ings, winners receiving the princely sum of 6s 8d in prize money. Frequent inundations of the course interrupted the meetings and alternative venues were sought. Desperate for dry and level ground in the winter of 1607/8, the organisers of the event incongruously laid out a course on the frozen River Ouse. By this time, regular racing was taking place on Acomb Moor, two miles from the city centre. Races were usually between two horses, individual owners staking bets on the alacrity of their own steeds. In 1633, Charles I brought his own horse to compete in York. It lost. The sovereign was not amused and successive monarchs eschewed the York course for another 300 years until Elizabeth II graced a meeting in 1972.

In the reign of Queen Anne, racing was switched to another swampy course at Clifton Ings. Proceedings became progressively more organised and the incentives for competition were improved with the donation of five gold plates. In August 1713, 'His Majesty's 100 Guineas' meeting was inaugurated. It proved a popular event in the sporting calendar of York, but by 1730 it was obvious that if racing was to continue and be expanded, a radically new, purpose-built venue was needed using the very latest techniques pioneered by the landscape architects of the day. The location of the new course would be the Knavesmire, a long, waterlogged expanse of reeds and coarse grass used for grazing and the execution of criminals. The capable York Alderman John Telford, a professional gardener and seedsman, was given the task of creating the new course. Within twelve months the work was finished. The ground was expertly drained, levelled, seeded and enclosed, and the new course was opened to fanfares in 1731. 'His Majesty's 100 Guineas' was the curtain-raising event, a bay horse named Monkey owned by Lord Lonsdale romping home to become the Knavesmire's first ever winner. Racegoers from across the county flocked to the event, punter Simon Scrope of Danby expressing the views of many when he wrote: 'Tomorrow we set out for York to see the new horse course, lately made on Knavesmire, and to join in the great goings of the week, the life of which no town or city can compare with for gaiety, sport and company all of one mind.'

Thereafter, York Races became part of the social calendar, the annual meetings becoming ever more colourful and exciting. But for many people, proceedings were fundamentally marred by a gruesome reality that had existed on the Knavesmire since at least 1379. Part of the tract of land that had, by the eighteenth century, become the resort of fashionably adorned ladies, was used for the accommodation of an altogether different type of beast. Known as the three-legged mare because of its pyramidal shape and triple posts, this was the infamous gallows, the site of which is

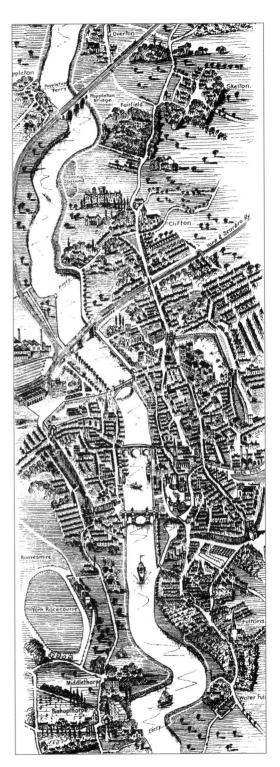

This stylised bird's-eye view of York clearly shows the convenient location of the Knavesmire and York Racecourse in relation to the city centre. *(From* Yorkshire Rivers – The Ouse *by Tom Bradley, 1891)*

marked by a modern stone on the Tadcaster Road. Until the practice was stopped and the contraption removed in 1801, Tyburn, as it was also known, witnessed the barbaric execution of hundreds of men and women. It has to be said that the hangings, disembowellings and ritual burnings were a popular and eagerly anticipated part of the York entertainment scene. Crowds could enjoy a good dangle in the morning, an exciting series of races in the afternoon and an evening's merriment at the theatre. The detached attitude to such inhumanity is readily summed up in one of the commonly heard sayings of the period: 'The assizes and the theatre always opened together at York, and it's common to hear the Tykes say "Eh lad; there'll be fun next week; t'play actors is coming and t'mens to be hung all at tsyame time."' Some people did complain, of course, and the outrage of the minority was given some prominence after the consort of George III – Queen Charlotte – pleaded for the executions to end.

Racing flourished on the Knavesmire. By the middle of the century, many titled and affluent members of the establishment began to develop studs and standards, and prize money improved, demanding race-goers clamouring for better facilities. Lord Rockingham, an avid 'follower of the fancy' himself, commissioned aspiring architect John Carr to design a grandstand to provide panoramic views of the races and by 1754, the stand was opened, bringing further prestige to York. In 1770, the city received a further boost to its international reputation when Knavesmire supporters formed the 'Ancient Fraternity of Gimcracks' – the first racing club in the world. The club's name was a tribute to an exceptional horse called Gimcrack that was immortalised in a painting by Stubbs. A flyer at just over 14 hands, the horse won twenty-seven of its thirty-five races although it was never successful on the Knavesmire.

The rules of racing evolved by degrees, the lack of formalised regulations, bearing in mind the large stakes involved, leading to much contrivance, confusion and cheating. On one occasion, two horse owners struck a bet to race each other over a measured mile. One arrived on the course and mounted up. Along trotted his opponent's horse with a professional, featherweight jockey in the saddle. The disgruntled man looked at the jockey and at his own expanding waistline. And he blustered and sighed. Then his Yorkshire instincts kicked in and he smiled, fingering his bulging purse and looking tenderly on the tiny figure of his 7-year-old son. Weighing in at 2 stone 13lb, the lad won by several lengths, George Stafford Thompson of Thirsk probably becoming the youngest ever jockey to compete in an official race.

Interfering with horses – nobbling, as it was colloquially known – was commonplace. The easiest way to slow a horse down during a race was to secretly overfeed the animal just before the start. Even highly trained prize bloodstock refused to shake a leg with a bellyful of carrots. Some tampering was cruder still. Fancied horse Miss Nightingale – she had finished second in the 400 Guineas Sweepstakes – was found dead in her stable just before her next outing, an autopsy discovering 2 pounds of lead shot moulded into putty balls in her stomach. Other tricks of the nobbling trade included the nicking of leg and hoof tendons with razors and the application of lethargy-inducing drugs such as laudanum. On occasions, one horse was substituted for another. Cheating became widespread and continued unabated until stewards intervened around the middle of the nineteenth century, when vets compulsorily examined horses' mouths before each race.

Racing at York attracted men and woman from all points of the social compass. The dukes, earls and other grandees came to disport their wealth and gain prestige. In their train were wide-boys, spivs, conmen and bookmakers who were all eager to cream off their own 10 per cents. Mostly, though, the crowds were made up of ordinary men and women who were out for a good time, many farm workers and factory hands walking upwards of 50 miles to get to the course. Many slept in Knavesmire hedgerows overnight. Losing your shirt or winning enough money to stand your friends a meat pie and a jug of ale was all part of the compulsion. Then as now gambling was the drug, although modern bookmakers could not possibly compete with one ruse perpetrated by the notorious Earl of March.

This eccentric gentleman frequented York Races for fifty years. As a young man he rode his own horse, Whipper-in, to victory and he gained a taste for the wager, any type of wager, often bragging that he could achieve near impossible feats . . . if the odds were right. His outrageous boast at a time when the only transport faster than a horse was as a human cannonball was that he could send a letter 50 miles within one hour. The bet was sealed, the Earl refusing to explain to the infuriated punters how he would achieve the task. He did it like this.

Just before a game was due to start, he engaged two entire village cricket teams with the promise that if all twenty-four players followed his instructions to the letter, he would regale every man with ale for a whole night. 'If it's not dangerous or illegal, you're on! What do we have to do now?' 'Oh, nothing much. You just have to throw a cricket ball around for a while.'

March took a standard ball and whittled out a hole in its centre to receive a letter addressed to the punters. The two teams were told to stand in a circle of a precisely computed diameter and to toss the ball with maximum speed between each man. The Earl, meanwhile, sat close by with a watch in his hand, making his calculations. 'Faster! Faster!' he urged, complaining when the speed of the ball was slowed by one left-handed player who fumbled with his catch. 'Drop out that man!' he shouted, encouraging the rest to even greater efforts. Round and round went the blurring ball for minutes on end, March's whip-like oaths spurring the by now tiring cricketers to frenzy. Mesmerised, dizzy, panting and exhausted, they groaned and pleaded for the ordeal to end but mad March drove them on. Oh, how gullible they had been! Oh, how the prospect of free beer had clouded their senses! 'Stop!' called the Earl at last, realising that his boast had been accomplished. Up he jumped, grinning insanely and shaking the hand of each cricketer in turn. Later, he claimed his winnings from the incredulous and reluctant punters who had been foolhardy enough to accept his bet. And he handed them that letter. The cricketers, of course, laughed and drank their fill.

Larger than life characters like March kept the race cards filled with their private racing duels in the early years of the Knavesmire but then in 1843, Clerk of the Course John Orton established York's first great fixture. It fittingly paid tribute to the Roman name for the city, the Great Ebor Handicap, later shortened to the Ebor, becoming an important annual event attended by thousands of race-goers. Three years later, the Gimcrack Stakes was inaugurated, the owner of the winning horse perversely having to donate three dozen bottles of champagne to the members of the Gimcrack Club. In one of the last of the classic horse-versus-horse races in 1851, Voltigeur, owned by Lord Zetland, was paired against Lord Eglinton's crack mount Flying Dutchman in the 'Second Clash of the Titans'. The first titanic tussle had gone Voltigeur's way in the Doncaster Gold Cup. 'We must have a return,' said Lord Eglinton. 'Naturally', returned Lord Zetland. 'A straight match on the best course in the country – York. Shall we say over two miles for a thousand pounds?' 'You're on!' In a race attended by thousands of partisan fans, Flying Dutchman gained his revenge. Later, the progeny of the two horses were paired to produce a number of flyers, including the 1875 Derby winner Galopin. York honoured the incredible Voltigeur with his own race in 1950 when the Voltigeur Stakes was introduced, and today you may dine in the Knavesmire's Voltigeur Restaurant.

At the beginning of the twentieth century, racing on the course was threatened in a dispute over municipal control and the rights of the pasture masters. A number of alternative venues were considered but none proved suitable as negotiations dragged on for four years. Eventually, the pasture masters accepted compensation for the loss of grazing rights and a new 35-year lease was agreed, allowing racing to continue, albeit under a long-term cloud. During the First World War, the course was appropriated for use as a military encampment and a Red Cross hospital, but after the fighting it quickly reverted to its peacetime role. In the exciting decade before the Second World War it was the jockeys' turn for stardom, the names of Gordon Richards, Steve Donaghue and Willy Carr stealing the limelight. The man who would later become Sir Gordon Richards for his services to horse racing won the Ebor four times and the Gimcrack three times. The names of his mounts were irrelevant. 'I don't care what he's riding' was a popular refrain that sent shock waves through the bookies. 'If Gordon's aboard I'll have a straight fiver on him to win.'

The Knavesmire was home to hundreds of prisoners of war until 1945 but with the huts gone and the first post-conflict classic looming, the racecourse prepared to receive one of the most massive crowds in its history. Ground conditions were unsuitable on Doncaster racecourse so the great St Leger was relocated to York. During the three-day meeting it is estimated that 750,000 people came to the city. On the racecourse, 'placing a bet was a work of art', thousands of people enjoying the ultimate tonic to the depressive aftermath of war by cheering home Chamossaire. Other notable winners that week were Gulf Stream in the Gimcrack and Wayside Inn in the Ebor, both horses achieving a tremendous double for owner Lord Derby and jockey Harry Wragg.

Racing continued successfully on the Knavesmire and its popularity was undiminished through the strikes and recessions of the 1950s and 1960s, behind-the-scenes activity in 1962 resulting in the forging of an extended ground lease that secured racing on the course until 2056. Given the new certainty, the race committee were able to embark on a major expansion of facilities with the opening of a new luxurious six-tier stand that provided reception facilities for VIPs, bars and a banqueting suite.

In 1970, the Gimcrack was won by the famous Mill Reef, an incredible horse that subsequently added the Derby and the Prix de l'Arc de Triomphe to his crown. Just two years later, tobacco manufacturers Benson and Hedges sponsored their Gold Cup for 3-year-old colts and fillies. The first running attracted the reigning monarch for the first time in 250 years, Elizabeth II enjoying the spectacle of Roberto triumphing over the 'unbeatable' Brigadier Gerard. Legendary jockey Lester Piggott came to prominence in that period. He loved the Knavesmire's wide galloping acres and he could often be spied in York between races, enjoying a coffee and one of his trademark cigars. Piggott won the Benson and Hedges Gold Cup in 1973 and 1974 aboard the filly Dahlia. He also rode Hawaiian Sound to a memorable win in the same race in 1978. Half owner of the horse, millionaire New Yorker Leone J. Peters, enthused: 'There's no European track to compare with York and the great facilities provided here don't exist on American tracks. It was York and not my interest in Hawaiian Sound that won me over to your English racing.' In that amazing year, Yorkshire racing was graced by the exploits of one of the most exceptional 3-year-old stallions in history. Trained at the Garrowby Stud near Bishop Wilton and owned by Lord Halifax, Chairman of York Race Committee, Shirley Heights won the Derby after triumphing in the Mecca–Dante Stakes in York. The following season, another household name – Sea Pigeon, ridden by Jonjo O'Neill – also entered the record books by winning the Ebor. And then in 1981 came one of the most memorable meetings in York's recent history when champion jockeys elect Lester Piggott and Willie Carson faced a showdown as the August meeting opened. Carson had accrued more wins than his nearest rival and looked set to add another to his tally in the Yorkshire Oaks riding Silken Knot. But in the home straight his mount buckled as one of its legs shattered, sending Carson tumbling into the path of five thundering horses. The jockey received a massive pounding, some spectators fearing the worst. He was rushed to hospital unconscious, a medical examination revealing fractures to his spinal column and skull, and a broken left wrist. Amazingly, a fully recovered Carson was back in the saddle the following year. He continued to win races and in 1990 he brought home Mujtahid in the Gimcrack Stakes, which by this time had become the richest handicap in Europe.

Ever a favourite racing venue, the Knavesmire was awarded the accolade of Racecourse of the Year in 2001 by the Racegoers' Club and the Racehorse Owners' Association, following another famous Gimcrack victory, the red and white colours of Sir Alex Ferguson and Manchester United crossing the line courtesy of the ownership-disputed Rock of Gibraltar.

Just three years on, the most important meeting in the city's history loomed large. While facilities were upgraded at the internationally renowned Ascot in Berkshire, the legendary Royal Ascot meeting was planned for relocation to Yorkshire in 2005, Lord Halifax saying: 'Let the world come to York.' Massive preparations for the five-day event were begun and work commenced on installing a new loop to lengthen the course. The economy of York was given a massive boost in anticipation of the meeting, wealthy race-goers clamouring for chauffeur-driven cars, helicopter services and even portable saunas and gyms. Hotel and lodging rates in the city and in nearby towns and villages soared to new heights, the Georgian mansion in Thorp Perrow near Bedale heading the impressive list of sumptuous accommodation at a rental of £50,000 per week.

Typically, though, the meeting opened under ominous skies and the rain fell on flat caps and tiaras, the Queen and the Duke of Edinburgh flying in by helicopter from the home of Lord Halifax at Garrowby to lead a list of celebrity punters that included the Duke of York, the Earl and Countess of Wessex, the footballer Michael Owen, Carol Vorderman the television presenter and Mel Smith the comedian and film director. Eventually the sun came out to crown a glorious meeting described by the noted racing commentator Brough Scott as 'just about the greatest racing festival ever run'. On the track, the lightning-fast Cape of Good Hope was flown in from Hong Kong to win the Golden Jubilee Stakes, and this set the seal on a wonderful five days. Some greedy 'get rich quick' hoteliers and service providers inflated their prices in anticipation of unguarded spending – one taxi driver displayed a sign saying NO FARE UNDER £10 – but many rooms were left vacant and goods and services were unsold. During the meeting, York itself was unusually quiet and business was much deflated. And as for the fashions . . . well . . . one couple wandered around in jeans, and two pals on a day trip from

'Oh. You don't understand one's accent? – Try this:– By eck, lad. T'bugger coom in fust. Fifty smackers or ah'll set t'corgi on tha!'

(Daily Mail)

Chineur wins the King's Stand Stakes during Royal Ascot Week 2005. *(York & County Press)*

Stockton eschewed top hats for flat caps, the general lack of sartorial elegance coming in for much criticism from what were described by one local punter from Barnsley as 'plummy-gobbed arse-heads from Ascot'. I myself, in my regular column in *Down Your Way*, was less reactionary and more seriously searching in my analysis. Commenting on the inability of Yorkshire women to wear the traditional racing headgear with anything like the aplomb of their more southern sisters, I noted the following:

> The female Yorkshire head has evolved over centuries, practically relegating any notions of fashion to a fancy stitch here and a knitted motif there. All head coverings had to fulfil the primary function of keeping the skull warm. They had to stop the hair contaminating food and, being dyed an eye-catching hue, to serve as a primitive global positioning system, allowing the master of the house, spying the hat from a distance, to shout out 'Ey up, love! My tankard's almost empty.' And hats had to be aerodynamic, allowing women to spend long hours outside in gale force conditions, carrying a sheep under each arm with no loss of mobility.

I hope my explanatory comments may find their way via Garrowby Hall to Buckingham Palace, so that the next time Her Majesty deigns to visit the Knavesmire she might come wearing more suitable headgear.

9

FIRE, BRIMSTONE AND FLOOD

As if war, rape, pillage, ritualised executions, murder, arson, mass suicide, bombings and accidents galore were not enough, Nature has to get in on the act as well to add to York's history. Has any other town in England had a more fiery and more sodden past? Sodom and Gomorrah were smitten and finally covered by the Dead Sea but plucky York, continually burnt and perennially flooded by the waters of the Foss and Ouse, remains eternal.

Fires have been a constant problem in the city since Roman times, the blazes in one building – the very symbol of York – illuminating its history like no other. The seven Minster fires that have engulfed whole forests of timber over the centuries are the stuff of nightmares.

The old chronicles record that the Minster was accidentally burned in 741. The Normans deliberately set fire to the building in 1069, its phoenix-like successor falling victim to an accidental fire in 1137 that consumed the greater part of York town, including thirty-nine other churches. In the middle of the eighteenth century, incompetence by a workman who was melting roof lead with a dish of hot coals, led to a further disaster, and then came a deliberate act of arson in 1829 that branded the name Jonathan Martin into the book of infamy.

A regular church-goer, the eccentric and mildly deranged Martin was accepted by the clergy and his fellow worshippers with Christian tolerance. Afflicted by a religious mania that caused him to berate the clerics with charges of hedonism, he regularly attended the Minster as part of his perceived divine mission, pinning grievances, like Luther before him, to the choir gates. He railed against the evils of wine, roast beef and plum pudding, suggesting in one edict that the very roof of the Minster would come tumbling down in anger at the excesses. He wrapped his missive in a stone and sent it crashing through a Minster window but the warning was tossed aside as the work of a crank.

Spurred on by a perceived call from God to destroy the Minster, Martin hid behind a tomb until the cathedral was locked and struck his flint on the night of Sunday 1 February. According to the arsonist, the cathedral organ was the manifestation of the Devil and that accursed instrument was targeted first. He stoked his fire with pages from prayer books and sheet music and escaped through a window using a rope.

York Minster has suffered a number of devastating fires over the centuries. This view shows the façade at the beginning of the twentieth century. *(From* The Enchanting North *by J.S. Fletcher, 1908)*

The fire burned slowly for five hours until the blaze was discovered next morning by a choirboy. He accidentally slipped on ice, looked up in horror at the smoke and raised the alarm, alerting a bungling crew of geriatric firemen who wheeled out the ramshackle Minster fire appliance from the vestry as the conflagration took hold. One hour later, the majestic organ was consumed, hot air drawn into the medley of pipes creating a cacophony of screaming sound akin to the snorts of some great whale. Molten lead poured from the roof and flames threatened the East Window, its scenes of the Apocalypse flickering in a sinister manner in the glow. It was obvious that help was required and a detachment of the 7th Dragoon Guards arrived with their own engine, further appliances coming from Leeds augmented by a private pump supplied by Beilby Thompson MP from his estate at nearby Escrick Park. For a time, it looked as though the whole of the Minster was doomed, but the collapse of the ravaged choir roof halted the spread of flame and the fire was brought under control.

The cause of the fire was first blamed on a wayward candle, but then someone recalled the threats of the idiotic fire-monger with the Northumbrian brogue who had ridden through the city on an ass threatening fire and damnation. 'Wanted' notices were posted and a huge manhunt was set in motion.

The Archbishop, meanwhile, surveyed the scene of devastation. Miraculously, the East Window had survived intact although its stonework was damaged. The organ was reduced to cinders, the archbishop's throne was gone and a fourteenth-century oak-vaulted ceiling had collapsed. But beneath the ash and debris lay a hidden treasure, exposed layers of archaeology, including part of the post-Norman structure, enabling the early origins of the building to be seen and properly recorded for the first time.

Martin was arrested on 6 February and brought to York for trial, the unfolding drama magnified by an endless stream of visitors to the prisoner's cell, the hullabaloo fuelling his growing sense of celebrity.

Seven weeks later, Martin appeared in court. The citizens of York had, of course, been regularly entertained at the assizes, but this particular trial was the legal event of the decade. Such was the clamour for entry into the public gallery that tickets were issued.

In the dock, the defendant appeared relaxed and nonchalant, offering a plea of 'My God did it!' The court was told that Martin had given five separate warnings inspired by the dream of a cloud that enveloped the Minster and by holy promptings to burn it down. In giving evidence, he was rational at times but, when examined on matters of religion, he became agitated and confused, denouncing 'fat and indulgent priests' and their lives of indolence and luxury. Martin faced the death penalty on a charge of criminal damage. Fearing the worst, his brother engaged the services of an eminent barrister, his arguments persuading the court that there was a madman in their midst. He was found guilty of arson but was spared the death penalty on the grounds of insanity. He spent the rest of his life in the Bedlam Hospital in London.

The people of York were outraged, popular animosity prompting the striking of a commemorative medal showing the incendiary in three positions – standing, sitting in chains and swinging by the neck from the gallows. Beneath the figures,

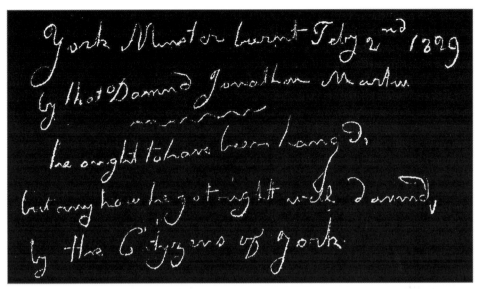

This anger-fuelled inscription was scratched into the pane of a Minster window by an irate workman after the incendiary attack of 1829. It reads: 'York Minster burnt Febry 1829 by that Damned Jonathan Martin – he ought to have been hanged, but any how he got right well damned by the Citizens of York.' *(LMA)*

the medal was inscribed with the legend: 'What I was. What I am. What I ought to be.' The increasingly rare medals are now collectors' items. Just eleven years after they went on sale, the Minster was burning again.

This time, the cause of the blaze was the inattention of a workman who, on the evening of 20 May 1840, left a burning candle below the bell chamber in the south-west tower. The flames spread quickly and, within minutes, the tower was engulfed as panic raged and young children were moved from nearby garret bedrooms to safety. The Lord Mayor ordered that fire appliances be brought by express train from Leeds, fire engines provided by the Yorkshire Insurance Company, the North of England Insurance Company and the Waterworks Company immediately attacking the fire, detachments of sabre-flashing guards and hussars holding back the anxious crowds.

To a tremendous roar of collective anguish, the tower roof succumbed and the ten great bells began to drop one by one to the ground, smashing their red-hot way through the intervening floors. For a while it seemed that the pumps were beating back the flames, but shortly before midnight the nave was engulfed, leading to fears that the entire Minster would be razed to the ground. With burning timbers falling all around, brave clergy and parishioners formed a human chain to carry priceless books and other treasures from danger, but the immense space of the central tower effectively acted as a firebreak and the pumps prevailed. Later, the distinguished Dean Purey Cust wrote the following: 'When the great roof fell and a sudden glare of fire lit up the smoke and darkness within, the great crucifix in the west window of the south aisle shone out distinct and beautiful.' Just days later, the clean-up operation began and within a few years the Minster was restored to its former glory, the fire-free Muses of the high altar breathing sighs of relief when the dragons of the Luftwaffe passed overhead in 1942 with their nostrils closed. But then, on Monday 9 July 1984, a lightning bolt tore down from heaven with incredible force, causing one of the worst fires in the Minster's history.

Just three days before the strike, the outspoken Professor David Jenkins had been consecrated in the cathedral as Bishop of Durham amid scenes of unprecedented hostility. According to some observers, his heretical remarks disputing the validity of the Virgin birth brought down the wrath of God. Some eyewitnesses reported seeing eerie flashes of lightning that played around the building for some time. The prelude to the strike – a low-powered electrical discharge known as corona – was followed by two devastating bolts of energy which melted the lightning conductors. Subsequent tests by experts at Leeds University showed that a metal electrical control box might have been hit by a massive pulse of energy causing a 'sideflash' fire that would quickly have ignited roof timbers.

The south transept took the full impact of the strike. Fanned by a stiff breeze, the whole roof was soon consumed in flames and molten lead began to cascade down even before the fire brigade arrived. Several firemen wearing breathing apparatus were despatched via a narrow spiral staircase to the roof area, hauling ropes so that hose lines could be dragged aloft. They were stopped by locked doors and the intense heat, and had to retreat as colleagues deployed scaling ladders to tackle the blaze from the outside. Ominously, the fire spread and more fire appliances were summoned, hose teams on the roof spraying the stonework above the Rose Window in a valiant attempt to cool the stained glass. Thousands of gallons of water were pumped from above and below, a water cannon in the vulnerable pit of the transept training a constant cascade upwards. By this time, a York crew had managed to penetrate the narrow space between the vaulting and the roof although their hose streams were deflected by the bows of the vault ribs and they had to retreat, blackened firemen passing groups of clergy and local residents who were desperately trying to remove items of value before they were lost for ever. It became increasingly obvious that the inferno would claim the transept roof and a decision was made to concentrate on defending the central tower. Yet more jets were brought to bear and hose lines began drawing water from the River Ouse.

At a giddy 198 feet, the central tower is one of the most awe-inspiring architectural creations in Europe, and it had to be saved. Such was the vast space, however, and the absence of convenient anchorages for the men on the pumps that the task seemed almost impossible until, at around 3.45 a.m., the burning transept roof collapsed and removed part of the danger. For the next few hours, firemen concentrated on dousing down and pumping out, and by dawn all the flames had been extinguished. Robert Runcie, the Archbishop of Canterbury, stood amid the ruins and uttered a stirring prayer: 'It will rise again.'

Within two years, the resurrection was well under way. Out of adversity had come the opportunity for architects to study the geometry and construction of

The aftermath of the south transept fire surveyed by Dr Robert Runcie, the Archbishop of Canterbury. (*Yorkshire Evening Press*)

previously hidden parts of the transept vault, some of the work dating from the fifteenth century. New designs, incorporating modern materials and fixing techniques, were drawn up, although, after much debate, it was decided to follow tradition and use oak as the constructional timber for the massive roof A-frames and the vault ribs. The Minster's twelve carpenters had a wealth of experience in working in oak, which was preferred to steel because of uncertainty about the metal's longevity (the roof had to last 500 years!) and the likelihood of contortion in a fire. All the latest and most sophisticated technological aids to assist fire prevention and detection were incorporated into the design, and the timbers were made oversize to allow for flame-inhibiting charring in the event of another fire. The works were fully completed by 1988 and, touch wood, nobody has delivered a really provocative sermon in the Minster in nearly twenty years.

Great empires and cities come and go but rivers run on forever, the waters that helped douse that last big fire in York bringing salvation and flood in equal measure. The River Ouse has nurtured the city since ancient times. Eighty miles from the sea at Ouse Bridge, which once witnessed a daily tide surge of 4 feet, York was built and sustained from materials and provisions carried along the river by boat, the lifeblood flow also providing fish, fowl, drinking water and the rudiments of sanitation. Together with the Foss, the Ouse also provided a protective defensive arm in times of conflict. It's little wonder, then, that York flourished within yards of the Ouse bank, a bank that has regularly overflowed.

Floods have been as common in York as rain. The Ouse above the city drains a vast area of north-west Yorkshire and receives the combined flows of the Swale, the Ure and the Nidd. Inundations have been frequent, especially in winter after seasonal storms, and many York buildings have been routinely swamped.

The dam that stood next to York Castle was in need of constant repair. It was swept away in 1315 by floods that destroyed the Castle Mills and 'softened the soil of the motte'. Rebuilt in 1316, it was damaged again and repaired in 1320, 1324, 1328, 1335, 1379 and 1428. The records only refer to York's more prominent buildings. No mention is made of the dwellings of the artisans and peasants who frequently scurried away like rats when the Ouse came seeping through their doors.

In 1564, a great flood swept through York and carried away the Ouse Bridge. Twelve houses precariously built on its structure were carried away. Successive floods in the years 1625 and 1626 reached record heights of 17 feet 7 inches. The torrent of October 1892 was not a record breaker but it was the first such York disaster to be comprehensively documented on film. After forty hours of incessant rain, the Ouse rose 16 feet above normal, transforming the city into an island. The sewage works was damaged, the gas supply failed, North Street and Skeldergate were completely submerged, and the gas lamps on King's Staith had water up to the ladder arms. Enterprising residents of the Walmgate area constructed makeshift bridges from planks and chairs and charged people for crossing. The scenes are beautifully recorded on glass slides in the Evelyn Collection held by the York Archaeological Society.

In the twentieth century, after one of the worst winters in British history, ice-melt transformed the Ouse into a raging torrent in 1947, devastating hundreds of homes and businesses. By this time, the widespread draining of land in the upper catchment areas and run-off from newly urbanised developments had led to unprecedented river levels, and flooding in York became more commonplace. In March 1968, hundreds of city homes and commercial properties were drowned just hours after heavy rain in the Dales. Ironically, by 1976, England was enduring its worst drought since 1720 and the Archbishop of York was praying for rain. The floods returned in 1982 and by February 1991 the Ouse reached its highest level for a century. Two years later, in May 1993, the waters again engulfed the cellars of the perennially damp King's Arms pub on King's Staith, although newly completed flood containment works helped to minimise the effects on other properties. The flood defences failed, however, to protect the city in

Catastrophic floods have been a feature of York life since the city was founded. Here, the police attempt to rescue an infirm resident in March 1968. *(The Press Agency)*

October and November 2000, when emergency crews in the city were put on a war footing.

The heavens had opened that summer; the rain falling on already waterlogged ground. The resultant flood took everybody by surprise, even seasoned hydrologists shaking their heads in disbelief as millions of tons of water poured through the city. Reaching 17 feet 10 inches above normal, the river level was at its highest for 400 years. Before long, floodwaters created an expanse of water larger than Windermere, 60,000 sandbags and the round-the-clock efforts of emergency services personnel, council workers, soldiers and legions of volunteers failing to protect the city. The King's Arms and Lowther pubs on the riverside were the first to flood, the new Queen's Hotel in Skeldergate and the City Mills complex drowning next. Before long, hundreds of residential and commercial properties were inundated. On the outskirts of York, the A64 trunk road became impassable and both rail and bus services were thrown into chaos. The famous Knavesmire gallops became a lake, some enterprising pub landlords pushing the boat out and starting a ferry service.

But the dark clouds had a silver lining for some local businesses. The Army Stores in Colliergate did a roaring trade in rubber boots and Anglers Corner in Walmgate enjoyed a similar bonanza in the sale of thigh waders. York was a city under siege, a one-word banner headline in the *Evening Press* – WATERWORLD – capturing the moment. But the Dunkirk spirit prevailed, a souvenir press publication entitled *Floods* selling out within forty-eight hours. Using gallons of fossil fuel, Prince Charles jauntily flew in to bolster morale but, like his gaffe-prone father, he put his foot in it by suggesting that the floods were the fault of society which had an 'arrogant disregard of the delicate balance of nature'. Cancelling an appointment with the Russian Premier Putin, Tony Blair also visited York early in November, the government subsequently pledging an extra £51 million over four years to assist with flood containment works. Two years later, flood victims were back in their newly decorated homes as Floods Minister Elliot Morley addressed 200 delegates at York's National Flood Forum. With impeccable timing the Ouse had just burst its banks . . . and it's still raining.

10
SWEET SUCCESS

Pioneering Quaker Joseph Rowntree was one of the first ethical employers in the world. His radical ideas changed everything. He left a blueprint for industrial democracy and social housing, a vast cocoa and confectionery business that at one time employed 4,000 workers, a model village, several trust funds, a community park and, for hundreds of thousands of schoolboys like me in every continent, Pavlov's dog reactions at the merest mention of his name: Rowntree. Just say the word and a million mouths salivate at the memory of those delicious fruit gums, hundreds of visits to the dentist doing little to dull the pleasure of dips into those colourful little boxes that continue to delight yet another generation.

Joseph Rowntree was born in York in 1836. A grocer's son, he was one of five children, the family living above a shop at 28 Pavement. An entrepreneur with a shrewd eye for business, Joseph senior realised that his shop was ideally located. The nearby market was the hub of daily life for both the citizens of York and for thousands of people in the countryside beyond. His shop would catch the passing trade at a time when coaches still rumbled through the city streets. The shop was open from 6 a.m. to 8 p.m., six days a week. On busy market days, opening hours were extended until 10.30 p.m. Trade was brisk and the atmosphere in the living quarters was stimulating and lively, twelve people, including brothers John Stephenson and Henry Isaac, together with several apprentice-shop boys, sharing the rooms above and behind the shop.

Quaker philosophy quietly influenced every facet of the Rowntrees' life. Hard work, honesty, sobriety, probity, frugality and simplicity infused the daily round, but the atmosphere of the household was far from solemn or sombre. How could it be otherwise with three young boys about? The boys were greatly encouraged by their accomplished mother. Years before the emancipation of women had been promulgated as a political principle, Quakerism led the way in allowing women unprecedented independence and freedom of expression. As well as running a loving, disciplined and an ordered household, the lady was a great organiser of religious and social events – particularly for the Society of Friends – and she excelled at oratory, helping her sons to participate in debates and to read widely. 'We had the reputation of being very wild children', wrote Joseph in a later memoir. 'I think that a stranger coming into the family would probably have been startled by the freedom we boys enjoyed.' The boys made kites, dabbled in kitchen chemistry and collected plants, butterflies and moths, their living quarters becoming even more cramped with the arrival of Hannah in 1840 and Sarah Jane in 1843. Two years later, the family moved to a larger house in Blossom Street. By now the strongly built 11-year-old Joseph had become a fully fledged Quaker. He attended the Friends' School in Bootham, his distinctive 'plain dress', consisting of a dark jacket and a wide-collared white shirt, drawing ridicule from other boys.

At the age of 14, Joseph was confronted with an event that would change his life. His father took him to Ireland, where he witnessed the scourge of the Potato Famine. Shocked at the hunger, destitution, death and the loss of all hope, he was fired to latent action, the memory of those one million fatalities inspiring his ambitions.

The Rowntrees moved house again while Joseph was still at Bootham. Nearing the end of his formal education, he jumped over a deep ditch – it was thereafter known as 'Joe's Jump' – and broke his leg. By the time the fracture mended, his schooldays were over and he joined the family firm, spending three industrious but largely uneventful years blending tea and coffee, weighing out butter and cheese and generally learning everything there was to know about the grocer's trade. After a third relocation to a still larger house which Joseph senior built as a retirement home on the corner of Bootham and St Mary's, Joseph grew restless. He visited London briefly in 1855, and was vastly impressed by the vitality of life in the city. Full of energy and ideas, he persuaded his father to allow him to return to London in 1857. He took lodgings and found a job as an assistant in a wholesale grocer's shop. He worked hard and became interested in politics, spending much of his leisure time listening to debates in the House of Commons. Integrating into the fellowship of Quakers, he made friends locally and became better acquainted with Julia Seebohm, the daughter of a friend in Hitchen. The lady would eventually become his wife in 1862. She died giving birth to the couple's daughter and Joseph married the dead woman's first cousin Emma Antoinette Seebohm in 1867.

Joseph returned to his father's employment, but in 1869 he joined his brother Henry as finance director in a business begun in Walmgate by an enterprising lady by the name of Mary Tuke in 1725. The business flourished, Tuke & Co., with Henry Rowntree at the helm, eventually becoming tea dealers and chocolate, cocoa and chicory manufacturers and, later still, one of the biggest confectioner manufacturers in the world. By the first half of the nineteenth century, over twenty York firms were producing confectionery products, names such as Craven, Terry and Rowntree coming to dominate the sector in the decades beyond. It is energising to examine how the tiny seed planted by Mary Tuke blossomed. For seven years this determined lady defied the powerful Merchant Adventurers' Company, which claimed a monopoly in 'foreign bought and foreign sold' goods. The company insisted on imposing fines for trading without a licence and repeatedly summoned Tuke to appear before a court. She resisted, developed her business, got married, became a widow, relocated her emporium to Castlegate, took on her nephew William Tuke as an apprentice and died in 1752, leaving all her by now considerable property to William. For three generations, successive Tukes expanded the business, Henry Rowntree buying the cocoa-making arm of the company in the year his younger brother was expanding his own horizons in London. Two years later, needing larger premises, Henry purchased an old iron foundry, a tavern and several cottages in Tanner's Moat for £1,000 and put up a new factory.

At the time Joseph joined the business, after seventeen years working for his father, the company employed just thirty workers but under his influence, it quickly expanded its operations and by 1873, its product lists included Rock Cocoa, Homoeopathic Cocoa, Iceland Moss Cocoa, Chocolate Powder, Hexagon Cocoa, Flake Cocoa, Chocolate Creams, Shilling Chocolate, Confectionery Chocolate, Sweet Shield Chocolate, Chocolate Drops and Penny and Twopenny Balls. By 1881, the highly popular Fruit Pastilles were filling the pockets of every urchin in the country, the manufacture of Fruit Gums, using real fruit essences, and iconic Jelly Babies, which led to ritualised oral decapitations that persist to this day, following shortly afterwards. Old photographs of the time show sweetly steaming vents and chimneys. Suddenly, everyone in York was a compulsive sniffer

Joseph Rowntree. *(City of York Council www.imagineyork.co.uk)*

and chewer. By 1882, the brothers had bought Simpson's Flour Mill on the Ouse to cater for increased trade, and just a year later their trade doubled. The mill was enlarged to facilitate the production of a new line – Elect Cocoa – and more capacity was introduced at the Tanner's Moat site that, by 1888, had a six-storey block of workrooms. In just seven years after the death of Henry in 1883, turnover rose 50 per cent but production methods were still largely primitive. Initially, there were only hand-stirred boiling pans and two coke-fired cocoa-bean roasters. The beans had to be laboriously lifted on and off the fires by hand and, in the absence of lifts, raw materials and finished goods were carried up endless flights of stairs. And if any component failed, the engineering department consisted of a man, a hammer, a cold chisel and several files! Gradually, though, new technology was brought in and the production processes improved.

In the lonely months after the death of his first wife, Joseph pondered on the essence of life, remembering his thought-provoking trip to Ireland. He worried about England's social decline, agonised over the recent cholera epidemics and railed against the horrors of the urban slums. Collecting statistics and analysing economic data, he produced a study showing links between poverty and crime, a similar analysis – *Pauperism in England and Wales* – following two years later. As an active member of the Temperance Society, he lectured on the evils of strong drink and became a supporter of the Liberal Party, his pioneering zeal for social reform finding expression in his own highly unusual and paternal management style that was often described by workers at Tanner's Moat as the 'J.R. Spirit'.

In the year of Joseph's birth the international slave trade had been abolished, but with the advent of the Industrial Revolution came a new and different form of oppression, profit-hungry factory owners becoming the new oppressors. Appalled at the exploitation, Joseph would set about creating his own framework for industrial harmony, and his personal influence on his workforce was immense. He led by example, recommending and never chiding, inculcating in his charges a sense of loyalty and harmony. Years before the concepts of industrial relations were formulated, he developed revolutionary ideas about working conditions and motivation, and he fostered skills enhancement and the unusual notion of teamwork. And he paid honest wages, even if the application of his payment procedures was a little eccentric. During the 1870s, workers were encouraged to scrupulously maintain their own worksheets and to keep records of the hours worked. At the end of the week, the foreman would pass round a hatful of wages, workers being asked to remove their dues. If, at the end of the operation, there were insufficient funds to pay the last man, all the money was returned to the hat and the process would begin all over again. Thoughts on welfare even extended to the firm's delivery donkey. Steam pipes from the boilers were extended into its stables so the beast could enjoy a steam bath! Some altruistic innovations did backfire. Keen to reward the hard work of his employees during the 1880s, Joseph organised a weekend's rail outing to Whitby. Many workers got hopelessly drunk on the excursion, and the police had to escort many inebriated passengers back home. Suitably chastened, their benefactor promptly cancelled further trips.

Encouraged by increased sales, Joseph decided on the need for a major expansion of his business and in 1890 he bought 29 acres of land off Haxby Road for the construction of a new factory. It would be a modern facility – single storey without stairs! – that would recognise the essential needs of the workers 'to develop all that is best and worthy in themselves'. Using a greenfield site, the factory units were designed around a tall chimney, a generating plant supplying light and power. The relocation from Tanner's Moat was organised in stages,

Rowntree's Cocoa Works from the air in the 1920s. *(City of York Council www.imagineyork.co.uk)*

beginning with the Fruit and Gum Rooms and the departmental offices, and in March 1897 the firm was newly incorporated as Rowntree and Company, with Joseph as the first Chairman of the Board. The other directors were his sons John and Seebohm, his nephews Arnold and Frank, and Mr J. Bowes Morrell. Theodore Rowntree, Arnold's brother, was appointed Secretary to the Board.

The directional mix was a powerful one. Chairman Joseph defined purpose and ethos, the younger members of the Board, like Arnold, who was in his twenties, introduced modernity and innovation. Driven by strict Quaker principles, Joseph always strove to produce top-quality goods at an honest price without the need for advertising. 'Quality Counts' was a slogan for the changing times of the Victorian period but times were changing fast, Arnold persuading his uncle to allow him to promote Elect Cocoa. Buying one of the very first motorcars to grace the streets of Yorkshire, Arnold fitted an oversized cocoa tin to its rear and had the vehicle chug the length and breadth of the major city streets. The contraption was unwieldy in windy weather and had to be transported to its destination by train but it proved a talking point – especially after it conked out in Sheffield and was issued with the county's first parking ticket. With cocoa sales soaring, Arnold took his sales campaign to the Oxford & Cambridge Boat Race of 1897. He hired a barge, festooned it with advertisement plates for the nation's favourite bedtime drink and had the vessel towed along the rowing course by a flotilla of mechanically propelled swans. Sales again increased. Back in York, Joseph had novel ideas of his own.

Like his father, fellow board member Benjamin Seebohm Rowntree was a born philanthropist. Animated by his father's earlier analytical work on crime and poverty, he embarked on his own studies, painstakingly investigating the circumstances of 11,560 York families. He discovered that 20,302 people – 27.84 per cent of the city's population – particularly in the notorious areas of Hungate and Walmgate – were living in poverty and with almost one-third of these in destitution. His researchers found jerry-built slums, contaminated water supplies, appalling sanitation, poor diets and malnutrition, drunkenness and low incomes. His 1901 publication, *Poverty: a Study of Town Life*, prompted York Council and Joseph Rowntree to action. By 1908, the council had begun to demolish the worst of the hovels; earlier still, Joseph Rowntree accelerated his own far-reaching factory reforms.

Rich and influential but unimpressionable and unselfish, Joseph was a man who would rather seek out a cobbler than waste money on new shoes. His one indulgence seems to have been the mind-expanding experience of foreign travel, but he was otherwise frugal in his appetites for the luxuries of life, preferring to expend large parts of his considerable fortune on his workers. Incrementally, he set the new millennium standard for industrial relations by introducing unheard-of improvements. He provided free education for workers under seventeen and instituted a five-day week with no appreciable difference in output. A factory library was installed. A social welfare officer, a doctor and a dentist were employed to provide free services to workers. Workers' councils were set up to advise on the appointment of supervisors and 123 acres of land were bought in 1901 to provide low-cost housing for workers. Disposing of his surplus wealth in 1904, Joseph established three trust funds. Two of these still extant trusts were devoted to

A Rowntree's chocolate advertisement from the Victorian period. *(LMA)*

educational and social improvements. The third was earmarked for the construction of his model village at New Earswick. This enterprise, together with similar schemes by other enlightened industrialists at Bournville and Port Sunlight, radically altered social housing policy for the whole of Britain. Not content with this, in 1906 Joseph personally donated £10,000 to launch a pension fund. By the end of the nineteenth century, his company had become an enormous success and a major beacon of industrial democracy the world over, employing thousands of workers.

Generations of York families were employed on the production lines, women with their distinctive smocks and flop hats making up large contingents of the workforce. 'I had a spell in the Cardboard Box making department and I got a certificate', enthused one lady. 'I worked in the Toffee Department, wrapping toffee', boasted another, 'and do you know, they were beautiful. And they did buttered almonds and things like that.' 'I was in the room where they covered everything in chocolate', added a third operative. 'It was called the Enrober Room. Now I loved that!' The boss also loved to sample-taste the confectionery and would often make impromptu tours of the workrooms, saying: 'I like to have a nibble now and again myself.'

Reading the accounts of the old production-line workers, with their tangy descriptions of fondants and sweets, sets the lips a-dripping, remembering that in those pre-E-number days all the ingredients were fresh. 'I used to go down to Wisbech in Cambridgeshire to get fruit', remembered the former head of the Coopering Department:

> I'd collect strawberries – I'd take about 500 casks with me. And I used to go to Maidstone in Kent sometimes – for cherries. I made the moulds for the chocolates in wood – 3 or 4 an hour. Then you had to finish 'em – put the whirl on the top and everything – and clean 'em up so's that when they put the blob of starch in with the cream and chocolate on top, it didn't stick.

Many of the workers were housed in the village of New Earswick – 3½ miles north of York – a delightful creation enhanced by a handsome school, a folk hall with an impressive red roof, quaint oriel windows, eccentric chimneys, rustic timbers and shady trees. The objective was to provide good-quality housing, 'artistic in appearance, sanitary and thoroughly well built', intended for employees earning around 25s per week. The scheme had to be financially viable. The new homes were built in short terraces in a revival Tudor style with gables and bargeboards. The architect was instructed to orientate the dwellings to gain the maximum amount of sunlight to living rooms. The new houses were popular from the start.

Running one of the biggest factories in Europe was an exhausting full-time occupation, but the ever-busy Joseph still found time to engage in politics. Vehemently opposed to the evils of drinking, he wrote several books and pamphlets on the subject – *The Temperance Problem and Social Reform* came out in 1900, followed by *Public Control of the Liquor Trade* in 1903 and the *Taxation of the Liquor Trade* in 1906. As an active supporter of the Liberal Party in 1907, he funded the establishment of the *Nation* – a periodical devoted to social reform. Three years later, he assisted in the purchase of the *Morning Leader* and the *Star* in order to thwart ownership by Conservative interests. He also opposed the Anglican Church, condemning its leaders for only lukewarm opposition to social injustice. And in another stand that anticipated the current debate about the usefulness of hereditary peers by a century, he pushed for the abolition of the House of Lords. Joseph Seebohm was essentially a gentle, thoughtful and considerate man thoroughly motivated by the ideals of a pacific Quakerism – but he was far from quiet!

The patriarchal Joseph was made a Freeman of York in 1911. Never resting on his laurels, he continued to work tirelessly, almost to the end. He only stepped down from the board in 1923, handing over the reins to his son and other relatives. Two years later, he was dead. In reporting his funeral, the northern edition of the *Daily Mail* devoted almost its entire front page to his good works, relegating news about an earthquake in New York to a small corner. But the benign empire he and his brother created lived on, and Benjamin Seebohm Rowntree became managing director in 1923. Benjamin worked closely with Lloyd George for two decades up to 1933, becoming Director of the Welfare Department in the Ministry of Munitions in 1916. Building on the reforms of his father and motivated by the potential of industrial partnerships, he piloted an early system of works councils and brought in widow's benefits and unemployment insurance far ahead of the times, becoming 'one of the great architects of the welfare state'. One guiding principle enunciated by Joseph formed the bedrock for all his actions, his father leaving a standard for industrial democracy that continues to exert a powerful influence on the world of work: 'There is no reason', he said, 'why the employer should be looked upon as a different kind of being from the workman.'

The Rowntree legacy lives on. The firm became Rowntree Mackintosh in 1969 and Nestlé Rowntree in 1988. And in the new millennium you can still buy those chewy gums. Now. Where are my false teeth?

An imaginative advertisement for Rowntree's Fruit Gums during the Second World War. *(LMA)*

11
EBOR GUM!

The archives of York are filled with monumental tales that shake the very ground of history, tales that fill your nostrils full of gunsmoke and set your heart racing. In this tribute to York, we have tear-jerking, gut-wrenching narratives aplenty, so let us stem the adrenalin rush for a while and take a more reposeful yet comical look at several less sanguine interludes in the life of this great city, beginning first on a good-to-be-alive spring morning in 1823.

The farmer and his pretty wife were very much in love. Arm in arm on that 17 May, they descended on York in high spirits, the farmer to attend to business matters, his country wife, with a wicker basket on her arm, rushing off agog down the fashionable Coney Street to buy candles, shortbread and buckles for her shoes. After purchasing her wares she turned her attention to the secret desire of her visit and became transfixed at the sight of the sumptuous dresses in the draper's shop window. She stood ogling for several minutes, wondering how she would look in one particularly divine Paris gown with its gorgeous ribbons and bows. Totally captivated at the sight, she never saw the man who crept up silently behind her. And she neither heard nor felt anything as he reached into her basket and made off with her handkerchief. Oblivious to the theft, she continued to gaze until a commotion near the Mansion House distracted her reverie and caused her to hurry along the pavement for fear of being caught up in an arrest by a burly constable.

As she scurried away from the scene, a distinguished-looking gentleman with a grey hat and a blue frock coat skipped after her, knocking his silver-knobbed stick all the while. Presently, he overtook her and politely raised his hat and bowed. 'Madam' he ventured, 'I regret I'm compelled to accost you in this manner – pray pardon the liberty. But are you not missing something?' Suffering from loss of breath and palpitations, the lady blushed and examined her basket. 'Yes, your handkerchief, dear lady', prompted the gentleman. 'It was stolen before my very eyes. I was standing near the draper's shop and I saw the villain come up behind you. The theft was of a trivial item I know but we cannot have thieves operating with impunity in the city of York preying on helpless womenfolk. Pardon my interference but I made it my business to follow the thief, to identify him to a constable and to affect his immediate arrest. Assuming you're not too disconcerted perhaps you'll accompany me to the magistrate's court – it's most fortunate that he's sitting as we speak and will deal with the matter with utmost expedition.'

The lady had little desire to get involved with matters of the law and would have willingly sacrificed the little handkerchief to escape from a predicament that might cause her long delay. And besides, the rendezvous time with her husband was fast approaching and he would be worried sick! But she had a stab of conscience and decided to follow the gentleman, hoping that justice would be lenient and swift.

The gentleman led the way into the dimly lit interior of the court, the lady wondering how an innocent peep in a draper's shop window had led to this. Successions of ne'er-do-wells appeared in the dock and were summarily chastised by the sombre-looking magistrate before the next handcuffed criminal was dragged in. But in an instant, that sunless and dreary place was transformed by ribald laughter, the magistrate glowing blood red and staring wildly at the culprit over his steel-rimmed spectacles. He was almost at the point of asking the sergeant of the court to remove the perpetrator of the jollity to the cells when our country lady cried out: 'Oh! Your Honour! It's the prisoner. Your Honour – he's my husband. I expect he's been up to his old tricks again. He's the most lovable tease in the whole of Yorkshire.'

'There, didn't I tell you!' cried the farmer. 'I ran off with her handkerchief just for fun. If it's an offence to steal something I've bought and paid for myself, I'll gladly go to prison for six months.'

'Hmm', muttered the magistrate, scratching his face, 'this rather alters the case.'

With that, the entire courtroom erupted into hysterics, even the glum old beak laughing until his eyes watered. The case was dismissed, the farmer and his wife leaving the court entwined lest the lady wander off and get into more trouble. The couple headed for Coney Street and walked straight into the draper's shop, the devoted husband marking the grand occasion of his liberty by buying his wife a certain little Paris ensemble with pretty bows. And it cost much more than a handkerchief. It cost so much, in fact, that he never repeated his little jape.

Money is a perennial subject for debate in Yorkshire and although there is no substance in the calumny that all Sons of the White Rose are congenitally afflicted by meanness – contrary to popular belief our infants cannot peel oranges in their nappies – it *is* true that Yorkshiremen will bet on anything. This fact is amply demonstrated by a wager referred to in an article published in a London newspaper in about 1880.

There was no meeting on the Knavesmire, one man's whippet had a broken leg, the other man's racing pigeons were grounded by high winds and the numbered snails that often perked things up in the bar of the Golden Gobbet pub by dashing across the floor to a spittoon had been innocently removed by a new cleaning lady, much to the consternation of the punters. 'What can we bet on now?' asked a grouchy William of Dick. 'I know', rejoined his inspired friend, 'we'll have a contest to determine who should succeed in adopting the most singular and original costume. Ben here can be judge. We'll meet tomorrow in the Castle Yard at noon. Is a wager of five shillings in order?'

The beaming contestants met the following day and whipped off their cloaks with a flourish and triumphant 'De-dahs!' William, whose stake money had burnt a hole in his pocket, was dressed in bank notes. Ten-guinea notes formed the

Self-effacing Tykes have always been blessed with a capacity for the sublimely ridiculous. This street performer in Stonegate, York, carries on the mad tradition. *(LMA)*

lapels and pocket-flaps of his coat; 5-guinea notes made up his waistcoat and collar-band. Further notes were pinned to his hat, its brim jingling to the sound of gold coins sewn in a little purse. On his back he had a sign proclaiming 'John Bull'.

Dick chose an altogether different and far more ingenious theme. On one half of his body he was dressed as a woman, the feminine guise extending from his rouged cheek to half a petticoat, one silk stocking and a single slipper. Her Siamese twin was a woolly-haired black man with one black boot and a spur.

Ben circled the contenders in silence, examining every facet of their attire. He should have acknowledged originality and imagination and awarded the 5s prize to Dick, but he adjudicated in William's favour instead. Dick was dismayed but he shrugged his shoulders and, with a little difficulty, reached into the malodorous recesses of his blackened breeches to retrieve his stake. 'Can't you be quicker about it?' chided a glum-faced William. 'Hang on a moment!' insisted Dick. 'As soon as I've cut it free, you can have it. But you've won . . . so why the black face . . . and what's the hurry?'

'Damn it, lad', insisted William. 'These notes aren't counterfeit, you know and the bank shuts in half an hour. Think about it! Every minute I'm stood here talking to you, I'm losing interest.'

William and Dick were descended from a long line of York punters whose bizarre bets raised the stakes in the art of gormandising. In about 1820, one hungry nose by the name of Mutton-Eating Billy Bandy took up the challenge by devouring a 10lb leg of mutton, two large bunches of turnips with a proportionate quantity of bread and a gallon of porter, all in one sitting. Suffering a slight bout of indigestion, the poor man retired to his bed and died. But he passed on his silver-plated toothpick to fellow gorger William Cook, Bacon Billy, whose attempts to eat 6lb of raw bacon in just one hour made headlines in the *York Courant* of 8 November 1825. Four pounds of streaky slipped down under the watchful eyes of the assembled throng, some consternation arising when the masticator asked permission for the remaining meat to be fried. After stern debate, the concession was granted, the onlookers settling their bets as Billy finished off his meal with a pound of cheeses and two penny rolls. 'Put your money where my mouth is,' proclaimed a triumphant Billy.

'I bet I can clear a dozen penny pies in as many minutes. Any takers?' The onlookers surveyed the prodigious paunch and drew the strings of their purses tight shut.

The reputation of William Cook spread far and wide and a month later he was back for a second exposition, the contest taking place in the bar of the Wind Mill inn near Castlegate Postern. His opponent this time was an 8½lb spitted duck complete with sage and onion stuffing and all the trimmings. He was challenged to despatch every morsel of the bird in one hour. Thirty-four minutes later he held a sucked-clean bone aloft to wild applause. Not content with this, he next called for a giblet pie, including the blood. Down it went, Billy wiping the gore from his mouth and asking for 2lb of cheese to settle a stomach described by the astonished reporter of the *Courant* as 'of the nature of a Boa Constrictor'. The reporter was there again in February 1826, lauding his hero as 'that most delicate

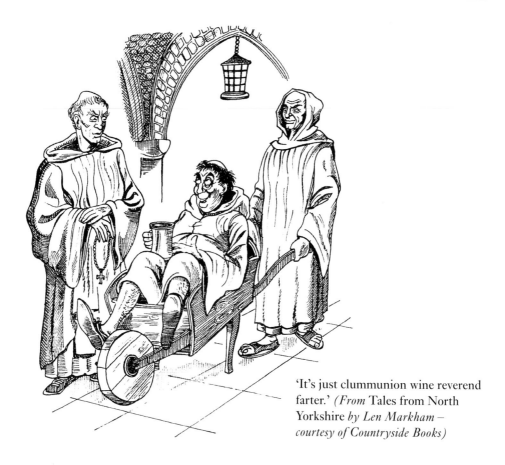

'It's just clummunion wine reverend farter.' *(From* Tales from North Yorkshire *by Len Markham – courtesy of Countryside Books)*

professor of mastication' who was backed to ingest, squeak and all, an entire 9½lb roast sucking pig. Young Pinky was no more after forty-two minutes, Billy delicately 'qualifying his pig with a penny roll washed down with half a pint of ale'. And still there was room for more! Billy called for Perky and wolfed the little fellow down in similar fashion. After that, all bets were off.

Bacon Billy was inspired by the legend of one of the finest trenchers in history. His name was Brother Jacundus, a monk at York St Leonard's Priory in the fifteenth century whose affection for hot pasties and 'holy water' created a legend that makes Friar Tuck look like an abstentionist. The jolly brother was recruited to the spiritual ranks in a curious way.

In celebrating the installation of a new Lord Mayor, he drank himself unconscious, waking up so befuddled and repentant that he signed on St Leonard's dotted line, the sober impact of his commitment only dawning when the vapours cleared. For almost twelve months, he stoically endured the rigours of the monastic life, weeping as his habit became ever looser and the fat fell away from his belly, only dreams of venison pies and tankards keeping him going during the long drought. Then, on the anniversary of his enrolment to the brotherhood, his resolve broke, the chink of tankards and the mirthful sounds of the annual York

Fair percolating through the priory walls and rousing him from slumber. With the devil on his shoulder reminding him that even Jesus had enjoyed a good drink, Jacundus purloined the porter's key and stole money from the prior's purse, escaping through the gates for a few uncaring hours of debauchery.

Liberated, he wandered joyously on an orgy of fun, enjoying rides and sideshows, gorging himself all the while on gingerbread and strong liquor. With the money in his purse almost gone, he bought one final jug and revelled in one last thrill, giggling uproariously and spraying ale from his mouth as the swing of a see-saw boat saw him rise to the heavens with the words: '*In dulce jubilo-o-o*. Up, up, up we go-o-o'.

But his final ecstasy was short lived. In the crowd, two fellow brothers who had been despatched by the prior, were ready to pounce and as soon as Jacundus returned to earth he was apprehended, this wobbling, slobbering, incoherent wreck having given up the use of his legs. Despite a year's dieting, the sinner had not lost sufficient pounds to enable the brothers to effect a removal on horseback without accusations of gross cruelty, so they borrowed a wheelbarrow, presenting the prisoner before the prior with the eyes in his sockets still spinning. 'This is disgraceful conduct, Brother Jacundus', denounced the prior, 'you deserve my sternest reprimand and the most serious punishment. How do you plead?'

'*In dulce jubilo-o-o*', chortled Jacundus. 'Up, up, up we go-o-o'.

Twelve hours later, when the fur on his tongue began to make Jacundus think that someone had planted a row of horseradish in his mouth, he woke up in total blackness. With only bread and water for sustenance, he found himself bricked up for eternity in the priory cellar in an oubliette, as was the monastic custom of the age. He was left to repent and die as dozens of fellow brothers chanted dirges and prayed for his soul. Jacundus thought this a bit much and began throwing his weight against the unseen walls. And lo! Let there be light! The party wall between St Leonard's and the adjacent building suddenly gave way and, in a cloud of dust, a surprised Jacundus tumbled into the cellar of St Mary's Abbey. After a while, he casually joined a group of his new-found brothers. Assuming Jacundus was a new entrant, the Cistercians, who were pledged to silence, nodded politely and went on with their devotions, later introducing the newcomer to the Abbot. Before long, Jacundus had integrated into the life of St Mary's, praising God for his deliverance and manfully eschewing the cheering cup. But on the anniversary of his ordeal, the devil pricked him again. The monk entrusted with the keys of the wine cellar suddenly died and Jacundus was immediately elevated to the post of victualler, the sight of so much burgundy breaking his resolve. He gingerly turned a tap and allowed a few drops of wine to drip on to his fingers. He licked with his eyes shut and sucked up a few drops more, purely, he persuaded himself, to establish that it was fit for human consumption. Then he poured himself a glass of the liquid and drank it down. Half a barrel later, he was hopelessly drunk. When he woke up for the second time in an oubliette, he was still singing.

Tragedy had recently struck the cloisters of St Leonard's next door. Its prior had died and the community was still lamenting on the loss, soulful requiems filling the air. Wishing to drink a final toast to his memory, the victualler had meanwhile been despatched to fetch wine. Nearing the cellar, he heard the strains of a notorious song and dropped his pitcher in utter astonishment and horror. From the exact position where Jacundus had been buried alive precisely one year before came the unmistakable strains of '*In dulce jubilo-o-o*. Up, up, up, we go-o-o.' The victualler ran all the way to deliver the news to the assembled brothers, who gazed up to heaven in awe and thanksgiving. Forgetting about the dead prior, they all rushed to the cellar and demolished the oubliette wall with their bare hands. 'Praise the Lord!' they shouted in unison. 'Look there! The bread and water is as fresh as ever. Truly, it's a sign from God on this otherwise sad day. It's miraculous. Come, Saint Jacundus, you are to become our new prior.'

Thereafter, the fortunate prior had to lead by example and he only rarely slaked his thirst in public. To show leadership, though, he introduced extra communion services and larger chalices, dying a happy man some twenty years later. The morticians, who prepared him for the crypt, had no need of embalming fluid.

York Minster is the most sober of places but, if you look hard enough, you will find mirth. Enjoy the humour of some of the roof bosses and the laughter of the misericords with their twisted bodies and contorted faces. They were for resting bums on, for goodness sake! And see the fun even in some of the tombstones, such as the seemingly solemn epitaph in the south choir aisle to the life of Jane Hodson, the wife of Phineas Hodson the Chancellor of York. Her monument, which records her passing, reads: 'She died in labour aged 38 on 2nd September 1636'. Nearly 400 years on, there is still nothing remotely comical about death, but looking down from her assured place in heaven with the hindsight of modernity, Jane must surely chuckle about her husband's crepuscular indulgences and his amazing choice of words. 'But it's in Latin!' I hear you complain. Let me translate.

> SHE WAS THE BEST OF WIVES
> WHO HAVING BLEST HER HUSBAND
> WITH NUMEROUS PROGENY OF BOTH SEXES
> AT LAST IN HER TWENTY-FOURTH LABOUR
> SHE FELL LIKE A SENTINEL ON DUTY
> WITH THE MOST PERFECT STEADINESS
> AND TRANQUILLITY OF MIND
> IN SO EARLY A PERIOD OF LIFE AND SUCH
> UNFAILING BLOOM OF BEAUTY
> THAT SHE HAD THE APPEARANCE OF A VIRGIN
> RATHER THAN THE MOTHER OF SO MANY CHILDREN

At one time, York was one of the most rat-infested, disease-ridden cities in Europe. In the dark years of the nineteenth century, it lost many residents to the scourge of cholera as a consequence of over crowding, poor hygiene and inadequate sanitation. Wonder then that one Elizabeth Burrell, a single pauper lady who rented rooms in Bedern in about 1819, survived to her dotage.

After twelve years, her plight came to the notice of the York Board of Health, an irate caucus of residents and an all-pervading odour that wafted over the precincts of the Minster like a nose-grabbing wraith, compelling the authorities to act. An inspector was despatched to Bedern to investigate. An able and conscientious man, he would have discharged his duties admirably but for one small problem. He could not get beyond Elizabeth's front door. For over a decade the lady had taken all manner of goods beyond the threshold, but according to the inspector, 'nothing ever came out until at last she could not enter her house'. In preparing his report, the inspector discovered that such was the prodigious amount of goods in the house that its occupier had 'for the last four or five years resorted to sleeping in a basket on the landing . . . and she has a great affection for cats'.

Forced to act in answer to the welter of complaints from Bedern residents – the long-suffering local mice would have added their signatures to the petition if they could have been persuaded to come out of hiding – in December 1831 the board decided to evict Elizabeth Burrell from her four rooms. And here is an inventory of what the bailiffs found:

700 pairs of old shoes.
50 tea-kettles.
A great bundle of mildewed old gowns.
A large stock of assorted rags.
Numerous rings and brooches.
An assortment of frying pans.
The skeletons of several cats and an untold number of live ones.
Several hundred putrefying fish heads (for the cats).

Seven whole cartloads of goods were taken away for disposal or auction, the sale of Elizabeth's entire store raising just 5s. Thereafter, the poor old lady was put in the charge of the overseer in All Saints' Church Pavement and she went on to live to a ripe old age, caring for the grateful church mice that forgave her everything.

And here as a sweet finale to this motley medley is a little story I recently heard on York railway station.

Three old, alcoholically propelled comrades were rounding off a reunion by recalling their exploits in 1944. Preoccupied with mutual hugging and backslapping, they hardly noticed the arrival of the last train to Edinburgh, a concerned porter taking pity on the group as, after a few moments, the express started to move off. Running down the platform he managed to bundle two of the old soldiers into a carriage but he had problems with the inebriated third. He was left standing on the platform, alone and confused. 'I'm terribly sorry, sir', apologised the porter, 'I tried my best to get the three of you on the train but there just wasn't time. That was the last train tonight. I'm so sorry for you.'

'Sorry for me?' replied the man. 'You're sorry for me? It's them buggers you should feel sorry for. They'd come to see me off!'

12

'LADY, YOU HAVE BEREFT ME OF ALL WORDS'

For the last fifty years she has starred in every form of popular entertainment with the exception of *Punch and Judy* and has gained every honour, including several BAFTA awards, an Oscar, honorary doctorates, an honorary degree, an OBE and a dameship. Uniquely, she has played almost every leading female part in the bard's considerable repertoire and has forged an international reputation for brilliant acting in theatre, television and film, her versatility embracing such diverse roles as Ophelia in *Hamlet*, Laura in the popular TV comedy series *A Fine Romance* and Iris in the film of the same name. A York doctor's daughter, beautiful and talented with a wry sense of fun, Judi Dench had everything but the name – a Yorkshire agent at the time might have said: 'You'll never get work with a handle like that, love; it sounds like something your father would prescribe for the itch' – but she went on demurely and unruffled with typical Yorkshire phlegm to conquer the world. And, true to her Yorkshire roots, she did it without any affectation or pomposity, taking her cue from her mother. One day in York the matriarch was among a group of actors, one boasting of his recent achievements. Unimpressed, she said: 'Pity he's dead.' 'Pity who's dead?' asked a bystander. 'His trumpeter.'

The youngest of three children, Judi was born in York on 9 December 1934. Peter, the eldest son, was destined to become a doctor, like his father. Jeffrey, the middle boy, would lead the way into the theatre. Their father Reginald was a vivacious and likeable Dorset man with a distinctive Irish burr and a kind manner. He spent his formative years in Ireland, where her met and married Olave Jones, Judi's mother. She was the disciplinarian of the family – quick-tempered and fiery. The couple, who shared an animated lifestyle and had an 'incredible sense of humour', lived at 54 Heworth Green, a Victorian terrace house on three floors, the accommodation providing living space and room for a surgery and a basement dispensary. Judi lived in an attic studio next to the maid's room. From an early age she was infected with the acting bug and was forever dressing up, giving her first performance at the age of 5 when she was a snail in a children's show at the

Rowntree Theatre. Reginald and Olave were keen theatre-goers and no mean thespians themselves. They became members of one of York's amateur theatrical groups – the Settlement Players. They entertained professional actors in their home, where Olave played piano, and when the York Mystery Plays were revived in 1951, they both became involved, encouraging Judi to appear as an angel.

Judi enjoyed a happy childhood. The family were great explorers and would visit Castle Howard and other local beauty spots on their bicycles. In the holidays they would go to Scarborough and Cornwall, Judi having fond memories of halcyon days by the sea before war broke out in 1939. In that year, she first went to school, the headmistress of Clifton Preparatory encouraging her students in all aspects of the dramatic arts. Judi remembers eating Yorkshire pudding with treacle every Tuesday and her irritated reaction at being recruited to play a fairy in a nativity play. 'There's no fairy in the nativity play – I'm just being shoved in,' she moaned. 'And I incited a chum . . . to dump frankincense on the baby's head. I felt very spiteful, especially as my doll was playing Jesus!' She and her family survived the war without mishap – Judi spending the night of the Baedeker Raid sitting on the Heworth Green stairs – afterwards resuming her rumbustious games with her brothers and other playmates, pranks such as blowing peas through a curtain rod at her father's patients confirming her growing reputation as a tomboy. In 1947, though, she put away her catapult and enrolled as a pupil in The Mount, York's Quaker school for girls.

A firebrand at school, she was chastised for spraying her dormitory with a fire extinguisher – for fun – and she would regularly take the opportunity to 'bunk off', making illicit trips home after games lessons had been cancelled during wet weather to enjoy tea and cakes with her complicit parents. But she found that the ordered and disciplined world of The Mount gave her a thorough grounding and a sense of responsibility, one particular teacher, a former professional actress known fondly as Mrs Mac, providing a wealth of inspiration. The curriculum gave Judi opportunities to act in school plays. She showed early promise as an actress and was much applauded and encouraged by her parents and her brother Jeffrey who was a student at the Central School of Speech and Drama in London. Perversely, though, she left school in 1953 with thoughts of pursuing a career in art or design, enrolling as a student in the York School of Art. She found the course less than stimulating and became disenchanted and fretful, arguing with her mother for what she remembers as the only such time in her life. 'She said I was the most intolerant person she had ever met, and at that point I think she was right.' Strengthening her resolve, she finally followed brother Jeffrey to London and signed up in September 1954 as a trainee actress, worrying if she had made the right decision. By the time her first term was finished all her worries would have disappeared.

Judi spent three busy and eventful years at the Central School, becoming an avid fan of live theatre in her spare time. She enjoyed all the top shows, marvelling at the performances of legends like Richard Burton, Paul Scofield, Michael Redgrave, Ralph Richardson and Lilli Palmer, she and her hostel roommate entertaining on a very limited budget but finding plenty of time for boyfriends. At Central she was taught all the rudiments of acting and about the importance of breathing, relaxation and voice projection. Her big break came at the Old Vic. Called with a string of other hopefuls to an audition, she was asked to recite excerpts from *Hamlet*. A few days later she was stunned to learn that she would be cast as Ophelia, acting alongside one of the country's leading actors, John Neville, who would play Hamlet. For her performances, Judi was to receive £7 10s per week.

Taking a break from rehearsals, Judi made a whistle-stop visit to York to appear as the Virgin Mary in the 1957 cycle of Mystery Plays. Sworn to strict secrecy about her debut role, she was bursting with excitement and although she did break the news to her parents, she kept the news from the local press, returning to London on the crest of a wave. The wave crashed in a series of less than congratulatory reviews. *The Times* referred to the production as 'lifeless'. The *Sunday Chronicle* commented on the raw recruit from Yorkshire, saying she had 'tripped over her advance publicity and fallen on her pretty face . . . A few years hard labour in proper obscurity will do wonders.' A more modest part as Juliet in *Measure for Measure* followed, other subsidiary roles coming her way during the Old Vic's Shakespearean season. In *A Midsummer Night's Dream*, Judi was an inelegant first fairy, her lifelong propensity to fall over drawing a stern rebuke from artistic director Michael Benthall: 'Miss Dench, will you try not to knock the other fairies over. You're coming in with your hands like a pair of finnan-haddies.' The theatre critic for *The Times* poured on the agony in reviewing Judi's performance as Maria in *Twelfth Night*, referring to 'a soubrette with a northern accent instead of a lady-in-waiting'. At the end of the season Judi became more deflated still. Benthall called her into his office with the news that her part as Ophelia would go to another actress when the company toured the United States. Tearful, she retired to her room and decided to have her lovely blond hair cut short. It has remained cropped ever since.

The Old Vic Company went first to France, Judi accepting the minor roles of the Princess of France in *Henry V* with Laurence Harvey, and Maria again in *Twelfth Night*. On then to the United States, Judi standing forlornly in the wings during performances of *Hamlet*. Although she fluffed her lines in her twin roles, the entire Old Vic repertoire received tremendous reviews, Judi enjoying the American experience and learning a great deal about acting from the tour. The season ended on a high note. The company were invited to Yugoslavia and Judi was restored to the part of Ophelia. This time she gave a more cultured performance. On one night alone in Belgrade there were seventeen curtain calls.

Back in London, Judi made her first appearance on television in a play called *Family on Trial* with Andrew Cruikshank. More small-screen work followed in Arnold Bennett's *Hilda Lessways* and in an episode of the legendary police series *Z Cars*. Judi continued her work with the Old Vic, the famous director Franco Zeffirelli taking charge of a controversial production of *Romeo and Juliet* starring John Stride with Judi as his lover. The play took a hammering from the critics but it ran for a record 122 performances and the public loved it. Buoyed by the success, the director took the play to his native Italy, where it featured as part of the Venice Festival, the organisers awarding Judi the Palermo International Prize as 'Best Actress of the Year'. The small but pushy Yorkshire lass had finally come of age. Bursting with ambition, she then took a mighty gamble. She severed her links with the Old Vic and took up an invitation to join the Royal Shakespeare Company instead.

It was a nervous start. A disparaging artistic adviser told Judi: 'If I'd been looking for Eliza Doolittle I'd look no further.' She shrugged off the criticism and took her acting to new heights, impressing her fellow actors, directors and critics alike with her talent and dedication. Dedication and total professionalism were required in spades for her next engagement – a two-month tour of Nigeria, Ghana and Sierra Leone with the Nottingham Playhouse, performing *Macbeth*, *Twelfth Night* and Shaw's *Arms and the Man*. Playing in makeshift theatres to excitable crowds and staying in dubious hotels, the tour was greeted with warmth and wild spontaneity, Judi and leading actor John Neville seeing the plays from a new perspective. Many in the audience laughed at Shakespeare's tragic lines, Judi and John sportingly getting in on the act and referring to themselves as 'the Morecambe and Wise of West Africa'. It was knockabout stuff in intense heat, John tearing off his armour after the final curtain call of Macbeth and ceremoniously urinating in the visor.

Back home, Judi was deflated by her father's ill health and by one of her most well-remembered flops. *A Shot in the Dark* opened well in Liverpool and Brighton but it struggled miserably in London. 'It was agony,' winced Judi. 'Nobody came. Nobody laughed.' Her dejection was temporary. In 1964, she joined the Oxford Playhouse Company. In that year, her beloved father died but she went on to play leading parts in five plays, finding time to tour and star in dramas for both television and film. Back next to Nottingham Playhouse for further renditions of what Judi did best, her enthusiasm for pushing the boundaries of her talent as an entertainer coming in 1968 with an offer to appear as Sally Bowles in the musical *Cabaret* at the Palace Theatre, London. There was only one slight problem. Judi Dench was not a singer. Dumbstruck at her recruitment to the vocal line, she promptly went out and got drunk, approaching rehearsals with great temerity. Assigned a singing tutor, she prepared for her big day with enormous energy, describing her first rehearsal with the entire orchestra as 'like an enormous pillow being blown up with you on top of it'. Before every performance she drank a bottle of champagne and gave a startling and intense portrayal that transcended her limited musical ability and proved beyond a doubt that she was an actress of boundless versatility.

As the plot thickened at a new season of the Royal Shakespeare Company's plays at Stratford, the effervescent Judi was centre stage. With astonishing creativity bordering on schizophrenia, she played mother and daughter parts in *The Winter's Tale*, the visceral juxtaposition of Hermione and Perdita delivering a triumph. Throughout that season her flair and sense of fun energised the whole company. 'The finest times I've known as a human being have been laughing, jet-propelled tears on stage with Judi Dench', enthused a fellow actor. 'I've never seen an equivalent performance', echoed the artistic director. 'Judi seemed to me to be at the very heart of the play.' A second visit to Africa followed, and by January 1970 Judi was breaking yet more theatrical ground with a tour of Japan and Australia. In comparison with the excitable audiences of Nigeria, theatre-goers in Tokyo and Fukuoka were stony silent, the typical oriental reserve only breaking down at the end, when there was wild applause. Onward to Australia and yet more adulation. But there was sadness as well. During the tour, Charles Thomas, a brooding Welsh actor who was prone to bouts of depression, killed himself. He was a close colleague and friend of Judi's and she was deeply upset at his death. The actor Michael Williams flew out Australia to be at her side. A romance with Michael had been germinating since 1961 after a tryst in Stratford. In the steamy atmosphere of the Antipodes it blossomed, Michael finding it difficult to tear himself away. He booked his return fare to London and Judi got on with her performance in *The Winter's Tale*. Imagine her astonishment when her heavily disguised boyfriend abruptly appeared on stage as a grotesque rustic. She froze rigid. After that, Michael proposed. 'Ask me again on a wet day in London', answered Judi.

In London, the couple were matched by the astute RSC's artistic director in a play called *London Assurance*. It was an unqualified success, the award of an OBE following in 1970. For a time, the lovers were estranged but a chance meeting in the Opera Tavern cemented their relationship and wedding plans were made. The knot was tied binding pragmatist Catholic Michael to Quaker idealist Judi in February 1971, the wedding reception taking place, with typical originality, at London Zoo. That season, they appeared side by side in the RSC's *The Merchant of Venice*, rounding off a fine year in a Christmas rendition of *Toad of Toad Hall*. Michael played Mole. Judi was a field mouse, a stoat and Mother Rabbit. Afterwards, the pair flew off to Japan for another tour, Judi returning home pregnant. Tara Cressida, known thereafter as Finty, was born in September 1972.

The products of loving homes, both Michael and Judi valued kinship and they were keen to provide a convenient base for their extended family, imaginatively persuading all three grandparents to move to a large house at Charlecote near Stratford. Dividing their time between the house and their cottage in Hampstead, they headed off in their different theatrical directions, returning back to Charlecote whenever possible. In the thick of the RSC's productions between 1975 and 1980, Judi rounded off a string of successes with her starring role in *Juno and the Paycock*, receiving shoals of honours for her achievements. Between 1980 and 1983, she also appeared alongside her husband in London Weekend Television's *A Fine Romance*, a BAFTA award for Best TV Actress underlining the comedy's huge popularity. And in 1982, the consummate Shakespearian specialist knocked everyone off their perches when she cavorted between the sheets with a risqué American in her role as the lover Barbara the TV film *Saigon – Year of the Cat*. Shot in Bangkok, the production was a logistical nightmare but Judi's talent, dedication and good humour in trying circumstances impressed everybody. At difficult moments she would infuse the proceedings with her usual irreverence and levity, suggesting that the entire cast should retire to the nearby coastal resort of Phuket. The director of the film was presented with a souvenir to remind him of the many setbacks, Judi embroidering a cushion with the words: 'Fuck 'Em'. The film was a winner but all the accolades failed to counter one of the most traumatic experiences of her life: her beloved mother Olave passed away in February 1983.

Watching the degeneration of Olave had focused Judi's own fears of death. She was terrified about the finality of dying and although she reluctantly acknowledged that there is 'a divinity which shapes our ends', even talk about an after-life could bring her to tears. Her confrontation with the inevitable was difficult and upsetting. She cried buckets but she came to terms with mortality and continued to work in her own inimitable fashion returning fittingly to her home town in July 1983 to receive an honorary doctorate of letters from the University of York.

Judi Dench is the finest genre actress of her generation. Renowned for her dominance of the theatre, she had devoted almost her entire career to playing to live audiences, latterly extending her popularity with television viewers, her role in *Saigon* promising an even brighter future on the wider screen. Her previous screen appearances, though, had hardly been the stuff of Oscars. Her first feature film was the infinitely forgettable *The Third Secret* in 1964. But more challenging productions were to follow that would propel her to international stardom.

In 1984, Judi for once in her life got to use her native Yorkshire accent in a film called *Wetherby* in which she appeared with Vanessa Redgrave. *A Room with a View*, *84 Charing Cross Road* and *A Handful of Dust* followed, Judi hitting the theatrical heights again in 1987 with a stunning portrayal of the Egyptian queen opposite Anthony Hopkins in *Antony and Cleopatra* at the National Theatre. The *Sunday Times* eulogised: 'British theatre at its spellbinding and magnificent best . . . both actors speak this soaring, voluptuous, difficult text with the finest of techniques which is based on artistic intelligence and true human feeling: two massive but golden performances from a golden age.' Shortly afterwards Judi was made a Dame of the British Empire in the New Year's Honours List, her fellow actors at the National spontaneously breaking out in song before a performance with 'There is nothing like a Dame'. Ever versatile, she then turned her attention to directing at the instigation of Kenneth Branagh, returning to BBC television in 1991 with *As Time Goes By*. As Jean Pargeter, a widow who meets a long-lost lover who went off to the Korean War thirty years before, she was to become a household name.

Jean Simmons had originally been earmarked for the role, but she was engaged elsewhere so Judi was approached. However, she was reluctant to sign up opposite the avuncular Geoffrey Palmer, having once been rudely propositioned by the man. There were difficulties over scheduling at first and Judi was unavailable, so the BBC decided to recast the part for another actress. Palmer, though, was determined to get his girl: 'This is bollocks!' he told the BBC. 'I don't want to do it without Judi.' The BBC relented and the show went ahead, Palmer saying: 'Acting with Judi is like playing football with Pele; it's a whole different league.' Philip Bretherton, the actor who played the slick and street-wise philanderer Alistair in the series, enthused: 'She can look at you and it's almost as if she has a switch somewhere and this light goes on. You think, where the hell does that come from. This light just zings across and takes your breath away.' The sexual and emotional frisson between Jean and Lionel kept viewers on their seats for weeks on end and the series was a monumental success, drawing an audience of over 12 million. The BBC immediately commissioned a second series.

But as one strand of fortune ascended, another reached the pits. Judi broke her ankle in a performance as Volumnia in *Coriolanus*. Typically the show had to go on; at the end of the run Judi took on a personally loathsome role as Helen in a play entitled *The Gift of the Gorgon*. She detested the play and found the Barbican venue depressing, a sad interlude nearly ending in complete tragedy when her Hampstead cottage caught fire. By this time, Finty was living there with two friends. In the early hours of the morning a burning candle set fire to the curtains and the occupants were lucky to escape with their lives. Judi was vastly relieved, but the blaze claimed many of her treasured possessions. She was despondent for a while but rehearsals for a new play cheered her up. Back in the saddle of live theatre she bounced back, her practical joking on the set of Chekhov's *The Seagull* prompting family friend John Moffatt to pen a cheeky poem that speaks of her vulgarity, rudeness and penchant for shouting 'Up yours!' Uniquely, Judi managed to combine laughter with gravitas, bringing audiences to fits of laughter and tears of sadness within the same scene. This ability was brought to perfection

Dame Judi Dench at a ceremony in July 2002 to mark the milestone of Jorvik Viking Centre's 13 millionth visitor. (*York & County Press*)

in her 1995 offering *Absolute Hell* and the musical *A Little Night Music*, that monumental year seeing her enlistment as the most famous spymaster in the world. Trembling in her boots, she was cast opposite Pierce Brosnan in the blockbuster Bond movie *Goldeneye*.

As 'M', Judi had a cameo role that was reprised two years later in *Tomorrow Never Dies* – but first to one of her strangest partnerships in nearly forty years of acting. In 1995, she was cast as Queen Victoria opposite a genius Glaswegian comic with a reputation for four-letter words and a wit that could take the paint off the Forth Road Bridge at 50 yards. Judi was enthusiastic about the part despite the warnings of the production company's managing director. 'I want you to know', he confided 'that Billy Connolly's first choice for Queen Victoria is Bob Hoskins.' 'That's all right,' answered Judi, 'it quite suits me to be Bob Hoskins' understudy.'

The anarchic pair clicked from day one and kept everyone in stitches on and off the set. Novice actor Connolly was 'carried along in her slipstream', Judi astounding film audiences across the globe with her portrayal of a demigod who was a combination of sensitivity, imperial power, feminine fragility, rage and tenderness. The impact of the film *Mrs Brown* was particularly strong in America, the *New Yorker Observer* reporting that her talents had been cruelly denied to audiences there. Judi was persuaded to attend gala premières in New York and Los Angeles, her queenly performance opening up cinematic doors that would eventually lead to an Oscar. Newspapers back home complained that the theatre had hogged Dame Judi's talents for too long. And Connolly's own career was given a tremendous boost by *Mrs Brown*. In appreciation of his co-star's help and friendship he presented her with a brooch. In return, 'she gave me a wee embroidered velvet cushion, which I'll treasure all my life'. She might have repeated the inscription made on the set of *Saigon*. Instead, the cushion was simply dedicated: 'To J.B. from V.R.' The movie attracted Oscar nominations and in the midst of acting in *Amy's View* – another drama that drew critical acclaim – Judi went to Hollywood, receiving the red-carpet treatment on the night of nights. She came away empty-handed but ecstatic, flying home to a fanfare reception at the BAFTA Film Award event at Grosvenor House where her portrayal as Queen Victoria received the Best Actress Award.

At the height of her popularity, she was almost immediately propositioned about a second regal film, the script of *Shakespeare in Love*, in which she would play Queen Elizabeth I, exciting her interest like no other. She jumped at the chance to play the fabled queen even though make-up for the part would take four hours to apply for only eight minutes' footage. But the blackened teeth, the wig, the platform shoes and the hideously heavy dress were worth it. At the next Oscars she won her award as Best Supporting Actress, her resounding fame propelling her along in *Tea with Mussolini* and *The World is not Enough*. The year 1999 ended in stardust. Not only did she receive an Oscar but a Tony as well for her part in *Amy's Girl*, becoming the first such double-honours winner in two decades. But the new millennium would bring incredible sadness, Michael, the love of her life, dying after a long illness with cancer. She nursed him to the end.

In November 2000 Michael received the papal equivalent of a knighthood. The Order of St Gregory would normally have been presented in the pomp of Westminster Abbey, but Michael was too ill to leave home and the ceremony was performed in his sick room. He died with great dignity and nobility shortly afterwards. Giving an oration at his funeral, Trevor Nunn, the director of the RSC, said: 'He told me once that his favourite line in Shakespeare was "Lady, you have bereft me of all words" – because when he was with Jude, he knew exactly the full extent of what Shakespeare was saying. A fine romance indeed.' In the mourning months, Judi received 3,000 letters of condolence.

After a few months coming to terms with her loss, Judi plunged into a busy schedule working on three film projects – *The Shipping News*, *The Importance of Being Earnest* and *Iris*. In the last she plays the writer Iris Murdoch, whose life was tragically cut short by Alzheimer's Disease. Martin Amis, who knew Murdoch well, was staggered at Judi's performance, saying: 'It is as if Dame Judi and Dame Iris were always on a metaphysical collision course. Her performance has the rarest quality know to any art – that of apparent inevitability.' On the strength of her performance she was nominated for an Academy Award for the fourth time in five years.

On her birthday in December 2001, before a glittering array of stars, Judi was presented with the supreme professional accolade for a lifetime in entertainment, the British Academy awarding her the coveted BAFTA Fellowship. In June 2005, her name appeared in the Queen's Birthday Honours List, Judi becoming a Companion of Honour for services to drama. Now into her seventies, she works on, the Chronology of Parts appended to her latest biography reading like a compendium of British popular entertainment. And all achieved without a trumpet. Her mum would be well pleased.

13

BARRY TONES

When John Barry Prendergast was born in York on 3 November 1933, the nation's wirelesses were lilting to the familiar tones of Louis Armstrong. But the midwife heard something else that day, the minute-old bundle in her arms emitting an utterly distinctive cry that was to change the sound of popular music forever.

John Barry was born with a silver tuning fork in his mouth, the influence of his father Jack Prendergast, a self-made show-business entrepreneur and theatre owner dubbed by many the 'Lew Grade of the North', setting a course that would lead to stardom. The son of Irish Catholic immigrants, Jack Xavier Prendergast grew up in Liverpool starting his career as a theatre manager. With a dynamic personality and an instinct that instantly recognised the potential of the fledgling film industry, he took a job as a cinema projectionist in Lancaster. There he met Doris, a classically trained pianist whose father owned a local repertory theatre. The couple were married and in 1923 their first son Patrick was born. Daughter June was the next addition in 1928, and John Barry – named in honour of the movie star John Barrymore – arrived five years later. By this time, his ebullient, ambitious, 'don't-stand-in-my-way' father had seen the potential of the fire-gutted Casino Theatre and Ballroom in Fishergate, York, and had decided to buy the property for redevelopment as a modern theatre and cinema. Jack shrewdly recognised the strategic location of his newly dubbed Rialto. As railway pioneers such as local draper George Hudson had ensured that York was an important railhead, Jack Prendergast reasoned that the city's easy links to the national network would encourage entertainers to visit. Jack moved his family to York and bought 167 Hull Road. In this modest home, John had his first experiences of city life. 'York is the most beautiful city in the world,' he said later, 'the most extraordinary place. But it's sad as well, and to live there – that's something else. One of my earliest childhood memories is of the sun going down, and it was if the whole town had gone to sleep. You could hear footsteps on the streets, and I used to think to myself, surely the rest of the world can't be like this! At the bottom of it all, I guess I also wanted to get away from my father. He was a very dominating gentleman.'

Within a few years, Jack's gamble had paid off. The Rialto became a roaring success, allowing the Prendergasts to move to the more opulent and elegant Georgian surroundings of Fulford House. By this time, the self-made tycoon had employed a full-time nanny to look after his children. He adopted the initials JX, ran a flashy car and extended his empire, running eight theatres with a discipline and authority that extended to his own household. Jack was never an emotional man and seldom gave praise, leaving his young son somewhat overawed and withdrawn but determined to succeed. Left to muse and indulge in his own fantasy world, John pursued his adventures in the privacy of his bedroom, the celluloid epics he enjoyed free in his father's cinemas inspiring youthful plots and party-pieces using toys as props and the strains of Sibelius, Ravel and Beethoven on the record player as background music. Fundamentally, the youngster was beginning to understand the mechanics of drama and music, the organic process of harmoniously juxtaposing one against the other laying the foundation for all his future success. When he was still in short pants, he decided he wanted to devote his life to music and become a composer.

John became a pupil at the Bar Convent Catholic Junior School opposite Micklegate Bar at the age of six. He hated the strict regime imposed by the nuns but he stayed at the convent until he started secondary education, narrowly missing death when German bombers targeted York on 28/29 April 1942. On the afternoon of that fateful day – the full story of the attack is told elsewhere in these pages – John was miraculously taken home by his father, who by this time had become head of the York Fire Service. High-explosive bombs hit the school and five nuns were left dead; John witnessed the conflagration from the safety of his suburban home. Within two weeks he was back in the classroom, the nuns stoically carrying on as normal as if nothing had happened. 'The really strange part of it is that my parents never talked about any of it either', remembers John. 'It was that Yorkshire thing of being very closed off.'

At the age of 11, John was sent as a day pupil to the upper-crust St Peter's School, swapping one set of disciplinarians for another. He found the strictures and the atmosphere dispiriting, claiming a lack of warmth, kindness and individuality. He hated St Peter's, subsequently reflecting on a perceived prejudicial attitude to his Catholicism. He also suggested that the school was elitist. Most of the pupils were drawn from the professional classes, and John concluded that his background, as the son of an impresario, was regarded with supercilious disdain.

John was academically bright and attained top grades in art, physics and chemistry, although his real love was music. In the macho environment of the 1940s St Peter's, a school which had a militaristic air and provided many officer-class recruits to the war effort, the study of music was regarded as vacuous and effete. Music figured little in the curriculum, but John managed to persuade his father to arrange private piano lessons. Rapped knuckles could have ended the musical dream right there but John persevered and learnt a valuable lesson. He had a natural affinity for the piano and showed great technique, but his lack of melodic memory and his unease in front of live audiences let him down, thwarting a career as a classical pianist. John realised his shortcomings, the reality nurturing the seed of an idea that would become his life's work.

John reached a crossroads at the age of fifteen. He had the option of staying on at St Peter's to join the musically impoverished sixth form or to go elsewhere, filling in his spare time by working at his father's theatres. With parental help he crucially chose to leave, one of Jack Prendergast's contacts, made through his staging of performances by the Hallé Orchestra at the Rialto, taking John on as a pupil. The tutor was the internationally respected Dr Francis Jackson, Master of the Music at York Minster. Jackson was a versatile musician, having led a dance band during the war and arranged big-band sounds. His eclectic tastes and his success – he made a piano recording of Billy Mayerl's 'Marigold' a few weeks before his eightieth birthday – encouraged John, who attended lessons every afternoon in Dr Jackson's home, where he was taught the basics of musical theory. Even at this early stage, the serious and rather restrained pupil indicated a desire to compose film music, the able doctor responding to John's declared ambitions by teaching him the fundamentals of harmony and counterpoint. The bedrock of a promising career was in place. What came next was John's musical *Borodino . . .* goodbye 1812 . . . and hello swing jazz!

Suddenly, John had a less snooty regard for contemporary music, the belting rhythms of Benny Goodman, Harry James and particularly George Swift prompting him to buy a trumpet and embark on a quest to discover the secrets of the brash new sound. Keen to understand the essentials of jazz composition, he asked JX if he might go to London to study with Swift, the man John regarded as the best trumpeter in the world. JX agreed and John spent two influential weeks in the capital learning as much as he could about the mechanics of jazz. In the evenings he went to the cinema and was captivated by the newly released *An American in Paris*, the music of George Gershwin leaving a lasting impression, the eclectic mix of jazz and orchestral strings suggesting a compositional formula that was, in future years, to help mould the distinctive Barry sound.

Back in York, John got his first break and joined local semi-professional dance band the Modernaires as third trumpet. He also began penning his own compositions and made a demo tape of his songs, using JX's friend Eddie Standring of Campbell Connelly as a sounding board. Standring was unimpressed and put a flea in the young man's ear. Disappointed but determined, John enrolled on a correspondence course to help him develop his writing skills –'The Schillinger Method' or 'Music by Maths' proving effective in analysing the structural fabric of composition. The notes kept on sounding and, taking advantage of the entrées provided by his father, who was on first-name terms with some of the biggest stars of the day, John sent his compositions to the likes of John Dankworth, Jack Parnell and Ted Heath. Dankworth was so impressed that he included one of the 18-year-old's numbers on his radio show. Parnell also gave some encouragement, suggesting that John might form a band of his own. But show business would have to wait. The year was 1952. National Service was compulsory for all young men of a certain age and John Barry was destined to spend three years as a bandsman. First stop, Richmond with the Green Howards. Second stop, Egypt.

Stationed 3 miles from the Suez Canal in a hot and hostile environment with plenty of time on his hands between performances and rehearsals, John took the opportunity to study his craft. Unlike his fellow bandsman who drank heavily to relieve the boredom, he eschewed strong drink, concentrating instead on widening his knowledge of musical composition. He was described at the time by close associates Terry Snowden and Mike Cox as being quiet and reserved and something of a recluse but he was admired for his dedication and good sense. After eight months in Egypt, he was sent to Cyprus. Again he used his free time to great advantage. He enrolled on another correspondence course run by Bill Russo, the orchestrator and arranger for the popular Stan Kenton band. John was one of only ten students and Russo, from his home in Chicago, gave him personal attention, setting compositional tasks and offering valid criticism. With long hours to fill between military duties, John had ample opportunity for musical experimentation and he had a whole band at his disposal, his fellow musicians proving more than willing to give an airing to some particularly offbeat chords. And then, capitalising on the momentum, he recruited five saxophones, four trombones, four trumpets and a euphonium backed up with a rhythm section, and formed his own impromptu band to play anything but Gilbert and Sullivan.

By the time of his demobilisation in 1955, John Barry was a competent musician and arranger. He returned to York and picked up where he had left off, rejoining the Modernaires and sending new but traditionally inspired compositions to Jack Parnell and John Dankworth. Suddenly, though, his ears were pricked to a new phenomenon. Post-war Britain was rocking to a fresh and vibrant energy. The word 'teenager' had been coined. There were record players and transistor radios in the shops, and coffee bars, pulsating with the raw-red sound of juke boxes, were on every corner. And outside the Rialto in York, much to the annoyance of JX, outrageously dressed youths wearing long jackets, tight trousers and crepe-soled 'brothel-creeper' shoes were congregating. They swayed oddly from side to side, greeted each other using a vulgar new vocabulary and sang badly, ululating disgustingly suggestive words from songs such as 'Shake, Rattle and Roll', and 'Rock Around the Clock'. John Barry loved it. Going with the flow, he quickly set up his own rock'n'roll band using a £5,000 loan from JX, and the John Barry Seven was born.

The band was innovative from the start. John purchased two state-of-the-art amplifiers and, being more adventurous still, a bass guitar, the Seven becoming the first rock band in Britain to include such an instrument in their line-up. The Seven practised hard, the ever-critical JX complaining from the wings about projection and style. The band's debut was at the Rialto on 17 March 1957, the performance later being described by John as 'hilarious'. The band melded together spurred on by John's drive for perfection. They introduced a choreographed dance routine into their stage performance in a style that Cliff Richard's backing group The Shadows would later make their own, and they recorded a demo tape, sending it off undaunted to Jack Good – the producer of the hottest TV show in town – the BBC's *6.5 Special*. Lacking originality, the demo tape was tossed on the pile that marked the graveyard of other hopefuls, but the Seven, undaunted, consolidated their position at the Rialto and other northern venues by continuing to develop their distinctive style. In the York audience one night was a London agent named Harold Fielding. Suitably impressed by what he heard, he offered the band a summer season supporting the astonishingly successful Tommy Steele at Blackpool. Before long, word filtered back to the BBC about the band and by September 1957, only six months after their first professional engagement, the John Barry Seven appeared on *6.5 Special*.

The band was a great success and other engagements followed. They toured the country in a beaten-up old bus and appeared alongside stars such as Tommy Steele, Paul Anka and Gerry Dorsey, who would later become the legendary Engelbert Humperdinck. In a traditional variegated mix, they also found themselves on the same bill as establishment stars such as Dave Allen, Larry Grayson and Max Bygraves, together with comedians, magicians and jugglers. But the blue-rinses in the audience objected to the ear-splitting sound of the rock and rollers. Something had to give. Before long, the teenage clamour for unadulterated live rock shows was met by putting on gigs in ballrooms. And here, there was ample room for dancing.

Rock and roll supercharged every teenager in the country and record sales hit new heights. John Barry, like other emerging pop idols of the day was determined to cut a disc, his first record 'Zip Zip' appearing on the Parlophone label in October 1957. With the distinctly untalented John on vocals, the record dived, the follow-up 'Every Which Way' also plunging to oblivion. Both records bombed but the failures steered John in a different direction. He began to concentrate on writing instrumental music, the new, heavily amplified electric guitar 'twang' sounds coming from America, pioneered by greats like Duane Eddy, setting him looking for a 'twang' guitarist of his own. Heading the ensemble of a newly reconstituted group was Vic Flick, John also recruited Les Reed on keyboard, saxophonists Dennis King and Jimmy Stead, bass player Mike Peters and drummer Doug Wright.

The new band produced more mediocre singles, John taking the opportunity to progressively record more of his own compositions. By this time, domicile in York, away from the capital's bright lights and recording studios, was hampering the group's progress, and John took the bold step of transferring his band to London. The lads took lodgings in the centre of Soho's red-light district in the Old Compton Street home of landlady Mrs Cotat, John's unique talents allowing him to secure what was described at the time as 'British pop music's plum job'. He became the musical director on Jack Good's new TV show *Oh Boy*. Classically trained, street- and business-wise and oozing with self-assurance and confidence, John Barry was a new breed of musical entrepreneur who uniquely spanned the gap between the old-time crooning generation and the raucous new stars of the pop era. Before long he was promoting the career of up-and-coming idol Adam Faith. Given his head, he arranged Faith's 'What Do You Want' in his own inimitable style with the Seven as a backing band accompanied by four strings. The record was a hit but Faith's rather weakly defined voice and unusual enunciation did not match the expectations of record producer Norman Newell. He famously commented to John on Faith's rendition of 'Someone Else's Baby': 'This is horrendous! He says "biyabee" instead of "baby" and sounds like nothing else that's out there.' By Christmas 1959, the record topped the charts and John and the Seven began touring with Faith and enjoying their own trappings of stardom. After dozens of takes and multiple bloodied string fingers – 'It sounds even better when you get down to the bone!' declared perfectionist John – the Seven had a hit of their own with 'Hit and Miss'. Afterwards, the stars of Adam and John rose in tandem and when, in 1960, Adam was offered the leading part in a pop culture film called *Beat Girl,* John got his first commission to write a film score. The burning ambition that first saw the light of day in the bedroom of 167 Hull Road would soon be realised.

The concept of using a pop musician to write the score of a feature film was revolutionary. Hitherto, such an honour was the preserve of well-respected classical composers like Vaughan Williams and William Walton, and many in the business resented the engagement of the relatively unknown and untried upstart John Barry. He set to his task between performances with the Seven, formulated his own way of working using a metronome, fought a battle with the recording studio over appalling acoustics and made himself unpopular. But he stuck to his guns and successfully recorded a soundtrack that was a soulful mix of all the music he had ever heard – jazz, atmospheric strings and the strident chords of pop guitars creating a musical mélange that set the scene for future scores that would so epitomise the James Bond movies. The score of *Beat Girl* was the first ever to be issued on a long–playing record in Britain. John subsequently landed the commission to write the music for the X-rated *Never Let Go,* starring Richard Todd and Peter Sellers and, before long, the more mainstream and genteel accompaniments to *The Amorous Prawn* and *Mix Me A Person.* More demanding challenges were soon to follow.

In 1960, the Seven were still touring and appearing on radio and television. John was working as an arranger for EMI, originating songs for dozens of singers and also finding time to write 'library music' (background instrumentals) for Chappell. The frantic pace never slackened, John taking on even more work by accepting a resident band slot on Brian Matthew's new Saturday morning radio show *Easy Beat.* And amid all the late nights and deadlines he found time to marry his Yorkshire sweetheart Barbara Pickard. After the ceremony, the couple shared a bottle of champagne and John went immediately on stage. A lightning visit to America came next. John was intrigued by the advanced pop arrangements and sophisticated new sounds coming out of stateside recording studios, and he was determined to replicate their success. He spent two weeks visiting Los Angeles, Las Vegas and New York, learnt numerous tricks of the trade and immediately began recording his only album, *Stringbeat,* a funky amalgam marrying the trademark pizzicato strings and twang guitar with the daring sounds of clavioline, glockenspiel, acoustic guitar and castanets. The album failed to set the music world alight, but just around the corner was the film score commission of a lifetime. In just a few months, Barry would meet Bond, James Bond, in a cinematographic collaboration that would amaze the film world.

The route that led to John Barry's association with Broccoli and Saltzman's *Doctor No* had as many twists and turns as any spy novel. For their score, the moguls engaged experienced songwriter Monty Norman but what he produced lacked vigour. They turned to the hip new kid on the block and he reworked the opening theme for a fee of just £250. The score was partly conceived through a long-remembered concert visit to York Minster as a teenager, St Peter's sublime and magnificent orchestra inspiring the use of an echo chamber to create an immense torrent of sound. When John saw the finished film for the first time he was surprised and annoyed to discover that his theme recurred throughout. This certainly had not been agreed with the producers and he complained and asked for more money. He got nothing extra, only an assurance that he would be considered for the next Bond film. But his involvement with the movie created a furore that, forty years later, still rumbles on today, Monty Norman disputing John's intellectual property rights to the 'James Bond Theme'.

After writing a notable jazz sequence for Bryan Forbes's the *L-Shaped Room*, John received two highly significant commissions that were finally to underline his arrival as a mainstream film composer. He took a long-awaited call from Saltzman and Broccoli and began scoring for *From Russia with Love*, working later, alongside unknown actor Michael Caine, on the score of *Zulu*. In between, he took on the lucrative role of managing the revamped Ember record label, recruiting his own acts and selling lots of records under the noses of the big boys. He also set up his own artists' management agency – Topline Artists. And in a scandal that rocked the entertainment world, he left his wife.

John and Barbara lived in a fashionable flat in London's Redcliffe Gardens with their young daughter Susie. By now, the composer was comfortably off and could afford the luxuries of life, including fast cars, fancy dining and the services of a live-in au pair – an attractive Swedish girl called Ulla. The couple had an affair and John left Barbara, scandalously setting up a new home with Ulla, who was soon to be pregnant. Within a few months, Sian was born out of wedlock. John's attitude reflected the social revolutions of the sixties. 'I guess I was one of the original sinners,' he later recalled ruefully.

Between films, John worked on the music for the Emmy-awarded TV special for ABC called *Elizabeth Taylor in London* and another similar TV extravaganza – *Sophia Loren in Rome*. He also re-orchestrated the theme for the British TV series *The Human Jungle* starring Herbert Lom, and even found time to set up his own company – Jinglewise – writing music for TV commercials. Remember the musical accompaniment to Silvikrin's 'The Girl with the Sun in Her Hair'?

By 1963, John's romance with Ulla had fizzled out. She went back to Sweden with their child and left John alone to indulge in a lifestyle that set the tone for the swinging sixties. An E-Type Jaguar, a trendy bachelor pad in Chelsea, designer clothes, A-list status and friends like Michael Caine, Peter Sellers, David Bailey, Shirley Bassey, Britt Ekland and Charlotte Rampling – the 31-year-old John Barry Prendergast had finally made it, gloriously casting off the legacy of JX. After successful tours with his own orchestra on the same bills as Shirley Bassey and Matt Monro, he accepted a seemingly uninspired invitation by folk singers Nina and Frederick to direct a short session of performances at the Savoy Hotel. The events surrounding this engagement were to stay permanently in his memory. During the session, John F. Kennedy was assassinated. The killing had a profound effect on him. He later moodily recalled his impressions of the event that shook the world in his 1998 album *Beyondness of Things*. A few days later, he had a more immediate encounter with one of his all-time heroes. As he was dashing down the Savoy corridors, he inadvertently careered into a man in a wheelchair. With a cut leg and a bloodied sock, John apologised to Winston Churchill and continued to his show.

The sixties let-it-all-hang-out party was in full swing and John Barry, in his trendy flat in Cadogan Square, was there in its midst, working feverishly at odd hours and living the no-holds-barred life of a superstar in the evenings. He had a flatmate in those days. An unknown actor knocked on the door one night in search of a bed. John let him in and Michael Caine stayed several months. 'The thing about John was that he used to write music at night,' recalls Caine. 'I would get up in a morning and he'd be there banging away on the piano having been there all night. Then he would go to bed in the afternoon and we'd have dinner together in the evenings. Then I would go to bed and he'd keep working.' John burnt quite a lot of midnight oil working on a new commission for the ebullient Mr Broccoli. The blockbusting 'Goldfinger', his first title song, was an enormous triumph, the belting chords of the amazing Shirley Bassey helping to steer the album to the number one spot in the American charts. Two million copies of the soundtrack were sold within six months, the album even eclipsing the Beatles' 'A Hard Day's Night'. John remembers his euphoria at the time: 'We were all young, we were getting the breaks and the Establishment had been told to go fuck itself.'

After *Goldfinger* came a score for another groundbreaking movie – *The Knack* – a voyeuristic, sexy, celebratory focus on the great generation divide. The film won the Palme d'Or. Afterwards, John renewed his collaboration with Bryan Forbes on *Séance on a Wet Afternoon* and *King Rat*, the war film about the appalling Changi Gaol taking him to Hollywood – at last. 'I want music which is ragged and awful', said Forbes. John produced a sound to match the tortured performances of George Segal, Tom Courtenay, James Fox and John Mills, introducing a little-known instrument, the cimbalom (a type of dulcimer, a triangular box with strings hit with sticks), at the heart of the score. Another great opportunity presented itself next. For the first time in his life, John was asked to write songs for a musical – *Passion Flower Hotel* – about a group of bored public schoolgirls who decided to set up their own bordello. Although the production was not a brilliant success, John fell in love with one of the show's vibrant young stars. He was married to Jane Birkin within months. At the ceremony in October 1965, the registrar asked the traditional question: 'Do you, John Barry . . . ?' Up pipes JX with the retort: 'What the bloody hell is wrong with Prendergast?'

The Bond movies created worldwide interest in the intrigue and excitement of international espionage and a series of similar films such as *The Manchurian Candidate* and *The Spy Who Came in from The Cold* followed in the early 1960s, John finding himself writing music to accompany the exploits of the antithesis of the super-spy – Harry Palmer – in *The Ipcress File*. The film starred his old flatmate Michael Caine. Bond was scintillating and sophisticated; Palmer was dull and lonely, John developing a score using the melancholy chords of the cimbalom that complemented Palmer's character precisely. Grouchy Saltzman was disparaging about the music at first, but John persevered and the film and its score, especially the opening sequence when the legendary noise of a coffee grinder was wonderfully interwoven with the introductory bars, was a massive hit. Another genre commission, *The Quiller Memorandum*, followed, John taking his cue from scriptwriter Harold Pinter to create gentle and melodic harmonies that were quite unlike anything he had produced before.

In a working life of immense year-on-year achievements, 1965 was to be even more monumental than most. With the accompaniment to *Zulu* in his musical locker, John was the natural choice as a composer for *Born Free*, a sentimental tale about African lions starring Virginia McKenna and Bill Travers. John was only lukewarm about the project at first but, focusing on the theme of freedom, he invented a sound and title music that captivated audiences across the world. The film was a triumph. John was accustomed to success but what came next blew his socks off. Actor friend Michael Crawford telephoned John in the middle of the night from the Academy Awards ceremony in Hollywood with the astonishing news that he had won an Oscar for Best Song. And then he paused. 'Ooh, but hang on a minute . . . the ceremony's still going on . . . wait . . . wait . . . oh my God, I can't believe it! You've just won another one! You've won Best Score too. It's incredible. You've just won two Oscars.'

With the reverberations of the double accolade still ringing in his ears, John became a father for the third time, Jane having just finished her own highly controversial venture into the unknown. John had married a highly sexy lady who would eventually record the unforgettably steamy 'Je t'aime, moi non plus' with Serge Gainsbourg. In her appearance in *Blow-Up* she really put her husband's credentials on the line. As a 'totally fucked-up Catholic' and a self-confessed libertine himself, he could hardly raise an eyebrow at his wife's nudity and he gave her the go-ahead. By now, another Bond bonanza was in the planning stage and before long, the automatic candidate for the musical direction of *Thunderball* was flying out to the Bahamas. And who will ever forget the dynamic chemistry of Barry and Tom Jones in that title track?

With a track record like his, John had met scores of famous people from the world of entertainment and elsewhere. In 1966, he took a call from one of the most charismatic of them all, American producer Sam Spiegel head-hunting him for a movie called *The Chase*. In the last two years of the decade, he worked on *Deadfall* and a film that allowed him to weave in all the musical impressions from his time in the historic heart of York. *The Lion in Winter* was set in medieval England and stared Peter O'Toole and Katherine Hepburn. 'I loved the chance to do a choral score', said John, 'because I'd studied choral music but rarely is there an opportunity to write that kind of material.' Combining the choral essence and tradition with modern instrumentation, which included the outrageous use of a Moog synthesizer, he created a memorable score. It scored well at the box office and won John his third Oscar. The triumph was overshadowed by a split from Jane. She moved out and he moved on, taking over a penthouse apartment in Alembic House overlooking the Thames. But he wasn't lonely for long, Jane's friend 19-year-old model Ingrid Boulting keeping him warm at night.

By way of complete contrast to *The Lion in Winter*, that man Bond pointed his gun at John again in 1969, *On Her Majesty's Secret Service* becoming the most grandiose genre movie yet. The film starring George Lazenby – by this time Sean Connery had become disillusioned with the part – was not a huge money earner but its finale was graced by a song that has since become a classic. Louis Armstrong was persuaded by John to leave his sick bed and sing 'We Have All the Time in the World' – a collaboration between John and lyricist Hal David. It was the last song the great man ever recorded. By the end of that amazing decade, John had reached the very pinnacle of his profession, married again, pushed the musical boundaries on a score for a television series called *The Persuaders* and gained an international reputation, culminating in his invitation by British director John Schlesinger to become musical director on *Midnight Cowboy*.

The Graduate with Dustin Hoffman had successfully pioneered the use of pop songs throughout the score and the formula was to be replicated in the new production. The search was on for a man who could source and coordinate material and reflect the often seedy and steely elements of the New York scene. Competition was fierce but John got the job. He supervised the recording of Harry Nilsson's memorable title sequence song 'Everybody's Talking', chose, produced and underscored the rest of the songs and wrote his own theme that captured the soul of New York in a haunting refrain played by virtuoso harmonica player Toots Thielman. 'I wrote the whole thing in an apartment on Fifth Avenue in twenty minutes, counter-melody and all,' said John, when one of the big-shot producers asked sardonically how a 'goddam limey ended up doing it'. 'Because a "limey" directed it and decide to use a "limey" composer,' retorted John. 'Because a "limey" knows how to look at New York. New York doesn't know how to look at itself, and Yorkshire doesn't know how to look at itself but John Schlesinger knew how to look at New York and he wanted me to do it because I knew how to look at it too. And *that's* why it was a success.' And a success it was, John making room in his display cabinet for yet another award – a well-deserved Grammy.

The swinging sixties, forever reprised as the most exciting epoch in modern times, went out with a bang and the film industry contracted reflecting national and international uncertainties. The new decade brought about a sea change in John's own career. He sipped several more vodka martinis with scores for *Diamonds are Forever* and *The Man with the Golden Gun* and worked on a number of musicals and minor film scores, one of his few failures, the musical *Lolita*, running for just twelve nights with losses of $900,000. In 1975, after a *tête-à-tête* with the Inland Revenue, he became a tax exile and spent a year in Majorca, filling in his time writing a jazz album. He recorded his tribute to the music that had so inspired him as a teenager and flew to Los Angeles to cut the disc. While there, he was offered the score for a TV special called *Eleanor and Franklin*. He accepted, got a second invitation to work on the score of *King Kong* and ended up staying in the US for over twenty years.

At the tail end of the 1970s, musical tastes changed and John found it hard to get work, music for films like *Saturday Night Fever* and *Grease* setting the tone that relegated serious composers to the sidelines. 'You couldn't get arrested,' said John. Somewhat disillusioned, he decamped to a mountain-top retreat in the Sierras for several months until he was lured back to his baton by a lucrative offer from the producer of *Game of Death*. And in 1978, he married his fourth wife Laurie.

After scoring the music for *Moonraker* in 1979, he relocated to Oyster Bay, Long Island, producing three of his most famous film compositions *Somewhere in Time*, *Body Heat* and *Out of Africa*. This sweeping and visceral homage to the savannah reflected the recent loss of his brother Patrick. It won John a fourth Oscar. With his tax situation resolved, he returned to the UK in 1983 and was reunited with Bond in *Octopussy* and *A View to a Kill*. He languidly signed off with his final Bond score in *The Living Daylights*, saying: 'It lost its natural energy. It started to be just formula and once that happens, the work gets really hard. The spontaneity and excitement of the original scores is gone, so you move on.'

In 1988, John almost died. He suffered a ruptured oesophagus after swallowing a health drink and was rushed to hospital to undergo life-saving surgery. He was critically ill for months but he survived and returned home to convalesce. Rest should have been his first priority but music was in his blood and he brought out his notepad and scribbled his own unique compliment to the mystery, dignity and aura of the native North Americans, producing another Oscar-winning soundtrack to the epic *Dances with Wolves*. On then into the 1990s with the typically Barryesque romantic themes for *Chaplin, Indecent Proposal, The*

John Barry hangs on to his hat during an honorary doctorate ceremony at York University, July 2001. (*York & County Press*)

Specialist and *The Scarlet Letter*, the 1998 non-film album *The Beyondness of Things* encapsulating nearly fifty years of musical experience sweeping from York to New York.

In 1997, the *Sunday Times* published an article that attempted to analyse the long-standing dispute between John and Monty Norman over parts of the soundtrack for *Dr No*, Norman subsequently filing a suit against the newspaper for defamation of character. The article in question annoyed Norman by referring to him as a 'little-known London musician' and a 'pop balladeer'. In contrast, Barry was called an 'Oscar winning composer'. In a tedious and complicated legal wrangle that ended up in the High Court, the matter seemed to have been resolved in favour of Norman but to all John Barry fans the verdict was academic, his thousands of supporters worldwide accepting an axiomatic comment made at the time: 'If Monty Norman wrote it . . . why isn't he still scoring the rest of the movies?'

At the time of writing (2006), John Barry, now in his seventy-third year, still lives in Oyster Bay. A retiring person not given to socialising, he continues to compose, retaining a tight-knit circle of friends, his definitive English accent and his lifelong love for Yorkshire and for his home city. And he has recently received the ultimate accolade of any citizen, becoming a Freeman of the City of York, the University of York also acknowledging his genius in the award of an honorary degree.

Multiple Oscar winner John Barry has received many awards during a lifetime devoted to music but it's the comments of his fellow professionals that he holds most dear. His friend and one-time flatmate Michael Caine called him '. . . one of the most brilliant film musicians in the world'. Jarvis Cocker praised his music saying: 'it seemed to really transform the world . . .' And the late Adam Faith, the singer he helped pluck from obscurity and make into a star, said: 'The way I saw my relationship with John was that he was the captain of the boat and he plotted the course and told us how to get there. If you were shipwrecked on a desert island, John's the sort of person you'd want to have around.'

14

WHAT'S IN A NAME?

In the world that existed before street signs, gazetteers, town plans, grid references, compasses and, if all else failed, a friendly policeman, orientating yourself successfully in any newly visited urban area was as likely as finding your way back along the proverbial creek without a paddle. One citizen's wooden hut was like every other and there were few landmarks to guide the way, only the most prestigious and distinguished stone buildings giving a clue to position.

In York, one structure rose above all the others to dominate the landscape, the Minster towering above its metropolis as a guiding beacon, the ancient thoroughfares spoking out from its centre like the filaments of a spider's web to give form, identity and a sense of location. Acolyte places of worship grew up in the shadow of this great cathedral and it is said that for centuries, travellers navigated their way through York steered by the forest of towers and spires that crowned its medieval churches.

Whip-Ma-Whop-Ma-Gate, York. *(LMA)*

Gradually, the street pattern took shape, influenced by the original layouts of the Roman and Viking towns, topographical features and the need to provide more bridging points across the Ouse, the names of the new routes metamorphosing over time to leave us with an esoteric lexicon of York that, in parts, is as intriguing at the Rosetta Stone. What do you make of Blossom Street, Dublin Stones, Footless Lane, Grape Lane, Trichour Lane and Whip-ma-whop-ma-gate?

As any visitor to York will soon notice, many of its street names have the common suffix 'gate' as an appendage, the term deriving from the Viking 'gata' meaning a street; hence Walmgate, Coppergate, Stonegate and Skeldergate. The history of such street names has been thoroughly investigated by expert philologists such as Swede Harald Lindkvist in 1926, A.H. Smith in 1937, Angelo Raine in 1955 and in more recent times by D.M. Pallister. All these experts agree that the vast majority of York street names are derived from Scandinavian sources, most of the streets being named during the reigns of the Scandinavian kings in the period 876–954 or during the final years before the Norman Conquest when Old Norse was the local vernacular. What is less certain, though (so my tongue is firmly in my cheek), is the exact meaning of the names: time distortions, interpretations and lack of evidence have led, in some cases, to differing suppositions, giving us a wonderful array of opinions and derivations.

Over 1,000 years on, the names of new streets are soberly decided by elected councils as a celebration of the achievements of local people, places or events. It was exactly the same in bygone days, Olaf the Glue, who boiled animal bones down by the River Ouse – 'turn left at the awful smell' – inspired the name Stickeegate. His friend Erik, who made decorations for Viking helmets and powdered bone for use in aphrodisiacs, gave us Hornygate. So, wander round the city yourself armed with that wonderful little booklet about the back alleys – *The Snickleways of York* – and enjoy an on-the-hoof history lesson guided by those modern equivalents of the towers and spires that even with the advent of satellite navigation are indispensable.

You can start at the Nags Head, a hostelry that needs no introduction on the famous Micklegate. One of York's principal thoroughfares from Roman times, this street is today famous for the so-called Micklegate Run. Mention this fact to anybody over 25 and they will stare at you in puzzlement, members of the younger fraternity who carry mobile phones in much the same way as Erik toted around his blowing trumpet explaining that the 'run' is a trial by imbibing. To complete the course, drinkers must visit every licensed premises in the street and consume one half pint of beer in each, reaching the end without falling over. The practice has debased this noble street somewhat, its name alluding to its greatness from as early as 1161.

To continue the tour, you must read on with frequent dips into my chapter about York pubs, following the route straight forward into Blossom Street. Ask for the sign of the Windmill. Is the street named after the wonderful cherry trees that at one time bloomed here every May? Resoundingly no! Ploxwangate! If you will pardon the expression, this simply means 'the street of the man who repairs ploughs'.

Back to the river next to find the enigmatic Dublin Stones. The name was originally given to a quay in the parish of All Saints' North Street describing the place where goods were trans-shipped for the Irish port. Footless Lane? Situated near to the watergate of St Leonard's Hospital, it was the place where disabled people congregated to seek alms.

I think you will agree that the resounding impression so far is that in deciding street nomenclature, our ancient Yorkshire ancestors, true to the tradition of the county, really did call a spade a bloody shovel. In the recent past, we have used innocuous and specious-sounding names to identify the very worst of urban slums and in this modern age we continue to employ universally non-offending language as a stricture of political correctness. They entertained no such vague nonsense in the twelfth and thirteenth centuries. You knew where you were with streets like Grape Lane.

If you had steered clear of Footless Lane after the curfew bell had sounded, you would certainly have made yourself scarce in, as it was called in 1329, Grapcunt Lane. The assumed allusion to fruit is a false one. Grap meant grope; cunt referred to part of a lady's anatomy, the notorious lane becoming the home of brothels. Trichour Lane, a lost alleyway off Fossgate, was another location to avoid like the pox. In medieval English, it was the street of the tricksters or cheats. Near its assumed location is the musically sounding Whip-ma-whop-ma-gate. There are no unsavoury surprises here. It is the shortest street in York, its much-photographed nameplate nearly outmeasuring its few short yards. In 1505, this gated entry into the city was recorded as Whitnourwhatnourgate following a popular derivation for whipping. The colourful story of its naming goes like this.

During a Mass in the nearby church of St Crux, a dog stole in and made off with a proportion of communion bread, the outraged congregation rising as a man to pursue the frightened creature into the street. Led by an irate priest who threatened excommunication and eternal damnation, the animal was cornered by the baying crowd, the priest urging the mob to chastisement, the sounds of a flurry of rods and sticks on the unfortunate creature's back giving us the most unusual street name in York. Just a few yards from its sign, through a narrow alley, is the tourist magnet of the Shambles.

The full name of this narrow old street is Flesh Shambles. This was the place where meat was displayed for sale on benches or shambles. The modern scene with the snaking rooflines and outreaching gables is the epitome of old English quaintness and gentility, but can you imagine the very different reality of life in 1586 when butcher's wife and martyr Margaret Clitheroe was led from her home at 35 Shambles barefoot to her execution in the nearby Tollbooth? She would have walked through a street rarely blessed by sunlight, picking her way alongside an open sewer between piles of excrement, sawdust and blood. A number of old streets like the Shambles have long since disappeared, one 'now you see it, now you don't' thoroughfare miraculously surviving the centuries and the attentions of the Luftwaffe in 1942.

Linking with the 2,000-year-old Stonegate – the Roman Via Praetoria – (it was the first road in the city to be constructed of stone) that led to the legionary headquarters, Common Hall Lane was the route from the fortress to the bridge

A pre-tourism view of The Shambles. *(LMA)*

across the Ouse. It was built over in the fourteenth century, enclosing a tunnel used for delivering building materials to the Minster. Laid open to the sky following the air raid, it was later partly reinstated to leave a narrow passageway running alongside the Mansion House.

Where next? Turn left at the top of Stonegate, having downed a swift half in Young's Hotel where Guy Fawkes was born in High Petergate (the highway dedicated to the patron saint of the Minster), and walk on to Bootham and Bootham Bar. These locations took their names from the booths erected by the monks of the nearby St Mary's Abbey for their weekly markets.

Finally, to complete your tour, head towards King's Staith, so called because this is where King Richard III embarked for his regular visits to his seat in Middleham Castle in Wensleydale, asking any policeman you come across in Coppergate – the street of the joiners or turners, the place of the copper furnaces or from the Old Norse word *koppr* or cup – to direct you to the Kings Arms. And if you see a philologist in there please defer the hospitality. The poor experts are confused enough!

15

GETTING AWAY WITH MURDER

There's a trio of murdered spirits whose souls are forever restless. They cry out from a lost millennium for a truth that will now never be told, the scales of virtue lying skewed and broken. Unseen and unaccounted, the crucial evidence that could have called the bloody perpetrators of those crimes to account is lost for ever. Decades on, one cannot help reflect on the time-dated nature of Justice.

The first of the awful crimes took place in York on 28 December 1904, the crisp winter morning riming the cobbles of The Crescent, a row of three-storeyed Victorian terraced houses that curved a fashionable arc off Blossom Street within rattling distance of the railway line. Two days after the double murder, apprentice gunsmith Fred Stone was busy at his bench, filing away. Casually looking up at a board set with hooks and assorted keys, he noticed that the cleaner's key to the door of the adjacent blacksmith's forge had hung undisturbed for days. What, he conjectured, had happened to Isabella Hewitt, the old lady who, as regular as clockwork, tidied the forge? Putting down his chisel, he wandered curiously across the yard to the tiny rented cottage that Isabella and 73-year-old retired North Eastern Railway Company engineer William Hewitt had occupied for seven years since relocating from Bridlington Quay. He knocked at the door of the oddly numbered 5½ without success – the lock had been secured from the inside – eventually shading his eyes and peering through the side window to see what was amiss. He was horrified at the scene. William Hewitt lay motionless on his stomach on the floor. Nearby on a sofa was the body of Isabella Hewitt, a bloody cloth hiding her mutilated face.

Fred Stone raced breathless to the nearest police station to report the crime, a grave Sergeant Bain calming the young man and effecting an immediate investigation. He rushed to The Crescent and gained entry to the cottage through a partly open side window to discover the two bodies. He carefully noted that William had been brutally assaulted, particularly about the head. His face was besmirched with mud and cinder ash, presumably carried on the murder weapon. The face of his spouse was even worse. On the right side, it was pulverised beyond recognition, bearing out Fred Stone's anxious account that brains were 'scattered about'. And Isabella's throat had been cut, drenching the murder scene in blood.

Sergeant Bain made his initial search of the house to find evidence, in a bespattered kitchen sink, of a hurried attempt at washing off bloodstains. As he began his enquiries among the neighbours, suspicion immediately fell on Harry Hewitt, a bastard adopted son of the deceased couple whose recent visits to their home had been far from harmonious. In April 1904, the police had been called to intervene – Constable Wand had attended – when the suspect had threatened the Hewitts in a vehement argument over money. At the time, one concerned neighbour had prophetically announced that 'they would get themselves killed'. The hunt was on as news of the terrible twin murders spread through a community that was agog with shock and speculation.

A description of Harry Hewitt was issued to every policeman in York and just a day later he was apprehended, wearing a distinctive billycock hat and a brown overcoat, as he entered The Crescent yard. An alert Constable Southwood, who had been instructed to guard the murder scene, accosted the suspect with the words: 'Who goes there?'

'Harry Hewitt' was the response.

'What do you want here?' persisted the constable.

'Oh nothing', answered Hewitt. 'Just looking around.'

With that, Southwood employed his handcuffs and led Hewitt to the police station, followed by a sizeable crowd. Alert to the situation, dozens of people gathered under the blue light to await developments.

Under interrogation Hewitt was non-committal, and at no time did he ask why he had been arrested. He spent the New Year under lock and key, and appeared, to answer the formal charge of 'Suspicion of Wilful Murder', in the Police Court on Monday 2 January 1905, the court hearing that the prisoner was a 40-year-old unemployed chemist. Unkempt, unshaven, taciturn and apparently phlegmatic in the dock – one journalist described him as a 'physiognomical mystery' – he uttered not a word as he was committed for a preliminary trial in the Magistrates' Court.

The following day, William and Isabella Hewitt were buried. Murders in the tight-knit community of York were uncommon at the beginning of the twentieth century and the city residents were appalled and traumatised at the deaths, an incredible 7,500 of their number lining the route of the cortege as it made its solemn way from the morgue to the York Cemetery Chapel to await interment. The costs of both funerals were generously funded by the Society of Engineers, ten of its pensioners, who had worked alongside William Hewitt, acting as coffin bearers.

The case against Harry Hewitt was circumstantial bearing in mind, with hindsight, the complete and utter lack of forensic evidence. The presumed murder weapons, a large wooden mallet discovered at the murder scene in a wash basket and a knife concealed in a rag, were both covered in blood, the abrasions and cuts on the bodies all being consistent with attacks from both weapons. Crucially, though, it could only be assumed that the blood on the weapons was that of the deceased. But what of the drops of blood subsequently identified on the clothes of the accused at the time he was arrested? In examining the marks on Hewitt's shirt and trouser leg, even the expert city analyst could not confirm a link. In the absence of any reliable scientific test, he had to admit that the blood could have been that of a chicken, a gory axe, again found in the cottage, suggesting that the old couple butchered their own birds. Faced with a paucity of hard evidence, the police pursued other lines of enquiry, seeking witnesses who claimed to have seen Hewitt immediately after the murders. There was a welter of information about the bad feeling between Hewitt and his adoptive parents, a cache of twenty-nine letters addressed to Harry Hewitt and discovered in a tin trunk in the bedroom of The Crescent cottage revealing that he had been born out of wedlock at Bridlington Quay in 1869. His mother was Mary Elizabeth Allen, who entrusted her son to the care of the Hewitts shortly after his birth. For a time, she paid £5 to the Hewitts every quarter for Harry's upkeep, but these payments ceased at the time of Mary's death in Collingham near Wetherby in 1877. Until 1883, a relative of Mary's continued the maintenance. Thereafter, only spasmodic payments were made.

In court, the prosecution made great play of the well-documented confront-ation between the old couple and Harry Hewitt in April 1904, Constable Wand reading the verbatim reports of the incident from his pocket book. Isabella Hewitt called the police in fright after her husband injured his leg in a scuffle. 'He thinks we're receiving money from his people that we ought not to have', she told the constable. 'I know you have', insisted Harry, turning to address Wand. 'One gets into queer streets sometimes. There wouldn't have been any trouble but for my father, who is in London. I know for a fact that they get money for me and they wanted to stop the clock on me but I wouldn't have it. They've not done as they ought or things would have been different.' This allegation was not borne out by the facts, evidence showing that no financial support had been received for Harry for some time and that the Hewitts were, in fact, in considerable rent arrears. The prosecution turned next to a witness, William Metcalf, who was alleged to have heard William Hewitt's cries for mercy.

Metcalf was an employee at the Station Hotel. He left work just after midnight on 28 December, passing along The Crescent where he heard a distinctive shout of 'Don't! Don't!' Stopping to listen, he noted a shuffling noise and the sound of a door slamming. Intrigued, he waited for five minutes, watching as a man wearing a billycock hat and a long overcoat left the yard and made off towards Micklegate. Under examination, Metcalfe could not positively identify the accused as the man in question. And his testimony was brought into further doubt by the evidence of the police surgeon.

Dr Harry Reynolds gave an expert opinion on how the victims died. He commented on the duration of the killings and their aftermath, suggesting that the brutal assaults on the old couple, the subsequent attempts to hide the murder weapons and to wash off some of the incriminating blood in the kitchen sink, and the actions of locking the door from the inside and climbing out of the window might have lasted in total not five minutes but at least half an hour. Isabella Hewitt died from five blows to the head – her throat was cruelly cut with a kitchen knife after she died – Reynolds suggested that she might have been intoxicated and asleep during the attack. Her heavy corpse, which the surgeon claimed could not have been lifted on to the sofa by one man, showed no signs of a struggle and there was an empty gin bottle close by. Eleven strikes of the mallet had accounted for William Hewitt. He was despatched in the yard and dragged inside.

Other witnesses were called, one explaining how, on the day of the murder, he met Hewitt in the Sun Inn at Long Marston. The accused bought him a pint of beer and he received, in appreciation, an ornamental walking stick presented to William Hewitt by his employers at Christmas 1903.

Throughout the proceedings, the scruffy Harry Hewitt was gruff and uncommunicative, while his defence counsel urged the court to dismiss the case through lack of evidence. The fifteen-man jury were not unanimously convinced of his crimes but, by majority, they found him guilty of wilful murder and he was sent to Wakefield Prison to await a full trial in the County Court.

The trial took place in York on 13 March 1905, a clean and presentable Harry Hewitt appearing in the dock to hear a recapitulation of the evidence presented at the Magistrates' Court.

No new information had come to light in the intervening months and, with a grinding inevitability, the spectre of 'beyond reasonable doubt' haunted the final moments of the proceedings, dashing the unshakeable conviction that the police had got their man. Harry Hewitt was found not guilty of the murder of his adoptive parents and was released as a free man. The case was closed. Agonisingly, just an atom of DNA might have put a noose around his neck.

The second of York's unsolved murders took place in the suburb of Tang Hall in September 1946. The period after the Second World War, was a time of renewal and optimism. In was also a time when children could enjoy unsupervised play, wandering freely without a care on the commons or in the shell holes to indulge in their own homemade fun. Fear of molestation or abduction was so uncommon in 1946 that the disappearance of 4-year-old Norma Dale on Saturday 21 September of that year hit the city like a bombshell.

No more than a toddler, pretty, intelligent and highly inquisitive Norma had light brown hair, rosy cheeks and an engaging smile. In good spirits, she returned that morning with her mother Frances Dale from a tap-dancing lesson. Back home in Rawdon Avenue, a fish and chip lunch was prepared, Norma's father, rugby league coach Cyril, sketching for his daughter once the dishes had been cleared. As ebullient as all children, Norma soon tired of her crayons and dashed out to play with her friends, and her father left with a friend to watch a local rugby game.

Dressed in a white cotton dress, white socks and distinctive black and red sandals, Norma broke off from her play to return indoors, snatching a rice cake from her mother and rushing off again to resume her games at around 2.40 p.m. That was the last time her parents saw her alive.

The custom of the time was to shout the name of your child from the doorstep, and Frances first called for her daughter at around 3 p.m. There was no response. Uneasy, Frances left her home and looked for Norma, several concerned neighbours joining in the hunt. By the time Cyril Dale returned home, panic had set in and the police were called, dozens of officers scouring the neighbourhood and the multiplicity of sheds, outhouses and gardens before dusk hampered the search. At 11 o'clock that night a radio broadcast was made asking for information about the whereabouts of Norma Dale. There were no replies.

Frances and Cyril Dale spent a sleepless night of conjectural torment hoping that dawn would bring some news of their missing child. It would not be long in coming. Dressed in his Sunday-best clothes, 11-year-old schoolboy Michael Duffy was playing truant from church and was idling down by the beck when a shape in the grass attracted his attention. Approaching a local coal merchant's lorry parked on waste land, he saw the easily recognisable figure of his fellow playmate and neighbour Norma, assuming from her position that she was resting. But she was dead and there had been no attempt at concealment. Then his heart was in his mouth. He noticed that one of her shoes was missing and that her face was a deadly blue. Terrified, he turned on his heels and sprinted to break the news to her stunned parents, afterwards returning home to tell his own father what had happened. His incredulous parent promptly clipped his ears for lying! A distraught Cyril Dale meanwhile confronted the scene and carried the body of his little Norma back home. It was less than a hundred strides to his front door.

Modern forensic science would have been deployed in all its painstaking complexity had Norma Dale been murdered today. A tent would have protected the murder scene, finger-tip searches would have been carried out in the vicinity and the corpse and its clothing would have undergone minute, protracted and exhaustive scientific examination. Even in 1946, it had been a great if an understandable mistake to remove the body, the policemen in charge of the investigation, Superintendent Cyril Carter and Inspector Thomas Capstick, recognising the problem by placing a life-size doll where the child had lain and belatedly cordoning off the area. Amid the confusion and conjecture, one thing was certain. The body had only recently been dumped in the grass. The area had been previously well scoured to no avail by the search parties and that very morning many neighbours had gazed across the land without noticing anything untoward.

The police soon established that the coal lorry owner, Fred Glover, who lived five doors away from the Dale household, walked to his vehicle to get a small amount of fuel to clean stains from his clothes just ten minutes before Michael Duffy made his fateful discovery. He saw nothing, his testimony enabling the police to determine that Norma's body had been dumped between 10.15 a.m. and 10.30 a.m. They were convinced she had been killed elsewhere, suspicions pointing a finger at someone with local knowledge.

Residents were interviewed and re-interviewed, dustbins were sifted for clues and even fire ashes were raked through in an attempt to locate fragments of the missing shoe, but by the day of the post-mortem examination on the following Monday, detectives were still clueless. Strangulation was determined as the cause of death, the autopsy mercifully revealing no signs of sexual assault. The time of death was fixed at around 3 p.m. on that Saturday, the rate of ingestion of the rice-cake snack giving an accurate fix on the exact moment of the murder.

Intensive enquiries drew a complete blank until a frightened 7-year-old local boy, Peter Bellwood, was persuaded to come forward with news that he had thrown stones into the beck with a little girl he thought might have been Norma Dale. He told the police that a stranger wearing a white-flecked overcoat and a trilby hat approached the pair and warned them about the dangers of drowning. He had assumed the man to be Norma's father. Coaxing the girl away with the promise that he would buy her an apple, he was said to have taken her by the hand and led her off. The police were sceptical of Peter's claims after he described Norma wearing a brown coat. She never owned such a garment.

At the inquest into Norma's death, the forthright coroner, Colonel Innes Ware, was hostile to the witnesses, making no pretence of his conviction that the murderer was in that very room. Reluctantly he gave a verdict of unlawful killing, concluding: 'As far as we have been able to carry out this matter, this enquiry has been exhaustive and we have done all we can, and there is no evidence on which the jury could make anyone party to the crime.'

Who killed innocent Norma Dale and why? Forty years on, a possible motive for the murder was revealed by a grown-up Michael Duffy, who aired his suspicions in an interview with the *Yorkshire Post* in 1986. 'I was only young,' he recalled, 'but I remember people saying that a lot of things were going on at the time. Men were going off with women that weren't their wives and Norma possibly heard something.' Gingered into action, a hitherto silent Frances Dale contacted the newspaper from her new home in Leeds explosively alleging that she knew the murderer. 'A married woman I knew told me she was having an affair with another man,' she announced, 'and Norma kept asking me about it. She had obviously overheard our conversation. She never missed a thing and I fear she might have gone up to this woman when her husband was there and started asking her about it. I bet the woman grabbed her to stop her blabbing and may have accidentally killed her.'

The burning questions are, why did Frances Dale keep quiet about her suspicions for forty years, and just who was that woman?

EVER-WIDENING CIRCLE OF QUEST

The police to-day are engaged in cutting the rough grass on the waste ground in search for clues. The area they have covered is becoming an ever - widening circle. Several samples have been taken from the area for forensic examination.

Superintendent Carter told the "Evening Press": "The police now feel that progress to date is satisfactory, but we are still not in a position to account

WHAT may prove to be a new line of inquiry into the mystery is shown by the fact that this morning the detectives, in the course of their questioning, were asking both men and women to illustrate how they would pick up and carry a young child.

for the child' movements between 2.40 on Saturday afternoon when she was last seen by her mother, and 10.15 on Sunday morning, when her body was found."

The murder of little Norma Dale made front-page news for days. This extract is from the *York Evening Press* for 25 September 1946. *(York Evening Press)*

16

THE BODY IN THE
SUITCASE

I was fuming. Catching sight of a suitcase and piles of festering rubbish on the grass verge as I drove along, I cursed, stopping briefly to remove a wind-blown plastic bag from my windscreen. 'They're turning the countryside into a bloody tip', I muttered, promising myself that I would contact York's Environmental Health Department that very day. But like numerous other local drivers, many of whom would have passed along that ordinary country lane between Bilbrough and Askham Richard near York in November 2001, I lambasted the unknown offenders and did nothing. How many fellow motorists – some of them must surely have spotted that incongruous suitcase in the hedge – must just have grumbled and driven on?

There was, however, something unusually arresting about that particular item of detritus. It looked too new and useful to be tossed away. And it seemed locked. So what was in there? Too-hot-to-handle silver plate from a country house burglary perhaps? Or was it a fly-tipped bundle of deadly asbestos or a consignment of illegal drugs? According to subsequent testimony, the suitcase was spotted in the hedgerow from as early as 2 November, but over a fortnight elapsed before, on the 18th, one curious man stopped his bicycle to investigate. He got the shock of his life.

The man pulled the exceptionally heavy suitcase from under the hedge and tried the locks. They were fastened. Suspicious about its contents, he telephoned York police, Sergeant Nigel Tottie and PC Richard Champion responding to investigate what was described as 'found property'. They too were intrigued about the contents of the suitcase and, mindful of the need to avoid contaminating potential evidence, they decided to leave it undisturbed and cordon off the area as a crime scene. Something permeated from the suitcase that autumn day. A smell and an awful presence alerted experienced Duty Senior Detective Chief Inspector Alan Ankers, who took charge of the investigation. He ordered that the suitcase should be left where it lay overnight pending a full forensic examination the following morning. This was carried out and the suitcase was taken to the mortuary of York District Hospital on Monday 19 November. The locks were forced open to reveal the partly clothed corpse of a young woman in the foetal position. She had been murdered.

Scanty details of the crime were reported in the *York Evening Press*, but a hurriedly arranged post mortem failed to identify the cause of death. Subsequent tests proved that she had been suffocated by an 'upper airway obstruction'. Local residents of Bilbrough and Askham Richard were baffled and shocked. 'This sort of thing never happens round here,' announced an anonymous woman. 'I can't believe that this is happening so close to our homes,' added another villager. 'I hope that whatever it is, it's not too gruesome. The police are keeping us totally in the dark about what's going on and it's causing chaos around the village with the road closed.'

The identity of the badly decomposed corpse was a mystery. The victim was very slender and only 4 feet 11 inches tall. She had been bound and gagged with distinctive adhesive tape and dumped in the rigid, silver-grey suitcase. Early enquiries revealed details of its manufacture and limited distribution by the Genova Company of Seoul in South Korea. It was produced almost solely for the home market and although some cases had been exported to Lebanon, none were available through UK outlets. DCI Ankers made a public plea for information. 'This is an horrendous crime,' he said, 'and no one deserves to end their life as an anonymous body stuffed in a suitcase and dumped in the bottom of a hedgerow. We intend to find whoever is responsible, but in order to do that we will need all the help we can get.' After engaging the services of a Glasgow anthropologist who carried out tests using 'red-hair analysis' as an ethnic marker, the police confirmed that the victim was of South-East Asian rather than Indo-Pakistani origin.

Despite four weeks of intensive police enquiries and widespread publicity the investigation was stalled. Reports of an unidentified man who parked a car at the crime scene on 2 November remained sketchy and uncorroborated, although some tantalising clues to the possible movements of the murder victim and the murderer emerged. The adhesive tape that bound the body was printed with an unusual motif of people and faces, investigators identifying its designers as the controversial artists Gilbert and George. Only 2,000 rolls of the tape were produced exclusively for the Tate Galleries' shops in London, Liverpool and St Ives. So far some 851 rolls had been sold. One of the purchasers was probably the murderer.

Frustrated police officers stared at their computer screens and reviewed a month of seemingly futile work. Across the world another screen watcher sought answers, a brother concerned about the disappearance of his sister posting details on an Internet website. And then, the long arms of coincidence combined. Byungho Im, a Korean police officer student at Leeds University, was idly scanning his own monitor when he chanced upon the website. He translated the information and immediately contacted the police in York. The rest was easy. All Korean nationals have their fingerprints registered in a central database for social security purposes. Details of the victim's fingerprints were sent to Seoul and, after nearly four months, a heartbroken brother finally traced his long-dead sister. She was 21-year-old Jin Hyo Jung.

Miss Jin was a student in Lyon, France. In October 2001, she left college, making a short sightseeing visit to London where she stayed in a drop-in hostel in Holborn run by a man called Kim Kyu Soo. Shortly before her disappearance, Jin sent her parents a last intriguing email referring to a 'kind' man she met in London. She explained that she planned to meet her 'friend' in Paris and travel on to Euro Disney. York detectives were soon on their way to the capital where they were confronted with a disturbing truth. Their London counterparts were also investigating the disappearance of a young Korean girl called Song In Hea. She had also been a guest at a hostel run by Kim Kyu Soo. And he too was missing.

Alerted to the distinct possibility of a double murder, the investigating officers pooled resources and set up an incident room in London's Edmonton Green Police Station. Their first lines of enquiry focused on the hostel premises and on the whereabouts of its manager. After numerous false leads, Kim Kyu Soo was finally traced to Canada. Meanwhile, his hostel and flat were vainly searched for clues to the disappearance of Song In Hea. According to witnesses, this student, who was studying hotel management at the Guildhall University in London, visited York by bus on 17 November.

Kim Kyu Soo unexpectedly and arrogantly returned to London on 17 January 2002 after a holiday in Canada. He was immediately arrested at a Bond Street Internet café and charged with the murder of Jin Hyo Jung. Under interrogation he admitted little, offering no explanation about the murder of his guest other than a vague suggestion that she had been seen in the company of a sinister black drugs dealer known as Do. Detectives proved this claim to be false. Detailed forensic investigations continued, one glaring mistake by the police teams being fortuitously uncovered by a workman. Called to carry out some work on 15 March in another of Kim Kyu Soo's haunts on Mile End Road, he noticed a nauseating smell and the appearance of large numbers of blowflies crawling from the confines of a panel. He telephoned police, who made the gruesome discovery

GRISLY FIND IN COUNTRY LANE

A dismembered body has been discovered in a suitcase abandoned in a country lane near York. After forensic examination, police have disclosed that the corpse was that of an oriental female. An extensive finger-tip search of local hedgerows on the outskirts of the village of Askham Richard is underway as part of an intensive murder inquiry regarded as the most bizarre in the history of the local force.

Typical headline reporting the discovery of the dismembered corpse. *(LMA)*

of a corpse hidden behind a cupboard. It had been sealed up and the handles removed. The body of Song In Hea had probably been hidden in the makeshift coffin for around four months. Kim Kyu Soo was charged on a second count of murder. Again, he refused to admit any guilt.

A motive for the double killing emerged, protracted enquiries revealing that the accused was heavily in debt. He had siphoned off funds from both victims' bank accounts after they went missing, the 32-year-old also being linked with the purchase of a suitcase that fitted the description of the case found in the York hedgerow. Faced with Kim Kyu Soo's steadfast refusal to cooperate with their enquiries, the police officers involved realised they would have to assemble a watertight case. For this to happen they would need to visit Korea and contact Jin Hyo Jung's family.

A video conference link was established between the police and family members in Korea, translators were employed to act as mediators and DC Lovell, an experienced Liaison Officer and member of the Family Protection Unit at Northallerton, accompanied the York team's visit to Seoul. Although the dead girl's father was a retired police officer with over thirty years service with the Korean force, he was not prepared for the trauma of losing a beloved daughter in such a brutal way, but DC Lovell, who was singled out for special praise by Detective Superintendent Ankers, performed with great skill, counselling and persuading the father and his relatives to attend the subsequent trial at the Central Criminal Court.

Months of painstaking research and compilation of evidence was presented to the court in a high-profile trial at the Old Bailey in 2003. Kim Kyu Soo was charged with two counts of murder. He admitted to the manslaughter of Song In Hea but denied both murders.

Jonathan Laidlaw QC outlined the case for the prosecution describing the accused as a 'seductive' landlord who may have killed the students for 'sadistic pleasure' to watch them die slowly. He graphically described to the jury how the victims would have endured agonising deaths by suffocation, saying: 'Each of the women appears to have been alive when this took place and one hopes they did not suffer long.' Laidlaw added that the torture could have been 'deliberately extended' to make the women reveal details of their bank accounts. A consultant pathologist told the court that Miss Jin died a 'very unusual death'; another expert Professor Christopher Milroy added that after a lifetime of experience he had never encountered a similar cause of death, describing the case as 'very, very unusual'. Refusing to take the stand, Kim Kyu Soo relied on his defence barrister to present his case. He claimed, with no great conviction, that the women died after energetic bondage sex-sessions had gone terribly wrong. But the evidence against his client was overwhelming.

Evidence was presented by telecommunications experts proving that Kim had travelled to York in a hire car contaminated with Jin Hyo Jung's blood. One of the rolls of the speciality adhesive tape discovered at his address was found to be similarly smeared and bloodstains on skirting boards, walls and on the edge of a bed were also proved by DNA testing to be those of the dead girl. Orange paint on one of Kim's T-shirts taken from premises in Toronto also matched that on the tape used to bind Jin's wrist. And evidence about the emptying of the victims' bank accounts was equally compelling.

Before a public gallery (and here is a most bizarre connection with a seemingly unconnected subject of this book) that included York's Dame Judi Dench who had earlier lunched privately with judges and City of London officials, the court heard that the accused was £17,000 in debt, having come to England in 2000 after his marriage collapsed. A dropout from an English course, he obtained work as a manager in hostels. After the murders, he withdrew almost £2,000 from Miss Jin's bank account. One withdrawal was made in Paris, 'creating the impression she was alive and well'. The other girl's account was robbed of around £1,300. Afterwards, Kim went on holiday to Canada, where he embarked on a month-long spending spree.

The trial jury returned a unanimous guilty verdict, Kim Kyu Soo showing no emotion as Judge Jeremy Robert imposed two life sentences. 'You snuffed out the lives of two innocent girls who believed you were their friend,' he said before a hushed Old Bailey. 'You did that in a way which must have been exceptionally distressing in the last moments of their lives.' In concluding the proceedings the judge described the entire enquiry as a 'Rolls-Royce presented case on behalf of the police'. 'I am very pleased with the outcome,' responded Detective Superintendent Ankers. 'I am very pleased for the families because now they can start to move on from the dreadful ordeal they have been through. Also, I'm pleased once again that North Yorkshire police have proved that we have some very skilled investigators who have worked in difficult conditions in company with colleagues from the Met on a difficult case and produced a top class investigation.'

The Metropolitan Police were also gratified at the outcome of the case, suggesting that had not Kim been caught, he would have killed again. But they posted a note of caution, pointing out that the murderer had travelled unmonitored across much of Asia, Canada and Europe. Details of his convictions were sent to police agencies in every continent on the basis that other victims might be identified. Kim Kyu Soo is just three years into his double life sentence but he may yet have questions to answer.

17

SOFTLY, SOFTLY, CATCHEE MONKEY

Deluged in a daily media torrent of sensationalised news reporting, we have become detached from and desensitised to death, only the more bizarre accidents and multiple killings warranting a place in modern headlines. And, in just fifty years, the reporting of the capital crime of murder has been largely relegated to the minor columns. The all-displacing news of murders no longer ripples through local communities with the threat of a tidal wave, occupying every edition, every thought and every conversation. But back in York in 1951 it was a different story:

MAN WHO LIVED ALONE FOUND DEAD WITH WOUND IN CHEST – YORK STABBING – YARD CALLED IN

The dramatic headline in the *York Evening Press* for Monday 29 January 1951 was greeted with horror and revulsion, scant details of the murder on the previous Saturday of 72-year-old former rugby league player Walter Wyld, from 199 Huntington Road, sending shock waves round the city. Described as 'quiet and inoffensive', the widower of two years had been cared for by a neighbour. She kept a 'motherly eye' on the pensioner and cooked and shopped for him in his 'spick and span' home. It was she who found the lacerated body with multiple stab wounds. Such was the overwhelming impact of the murder on the community and on local police resources that Scotland Yard was immediately alerted. And who stepped off the King's Cross train that Monday morning to lead the investigations? It was none other than a man the underworld had dubbed 'Charlie Artful', whose motto was 'Softly, softly, catchee monkey'. By his own later admission in his memoirs that spanned a career of thirty-two years, it was to be Detective Superintendent John Capstick's toughest case for the unlikeliest of reasons.

Assisted by Sergeant Plater of the metropolitan force and Superintendent C.T.G. Carter and Inspector E. Wild of the York police, Capstick immediately ordered officers to interview every householder on Huntington Road, asking for information about suspicious characters or a possible murder weapon. In enquiries hampered by 29 degrees of frost and thick fog, they also questioned bus drivers and conductors whose vehicles passed along the road at the projected time of the murder. Meanwhile, the official report of the pathologist was awaited from the Forensic Laboratory in Wakefield.

The next edition of the local newspaper had more banner headlines, John James Abbott, a friend who had known Walter Wyld for sixteen years, lamenting: 'His death came as a terrible shock to me. I cannot believe it. If someone has killed him all I can think is that they were after the money he told me he kept in the house. He used to say that he could put his hand on £50 or £100 if he wanted to.' And the murdered man's access to ready cash was no secret. He supplemented his pension with regular earnings from moonlighting as a jobbing joiner and for 25 years he had earned extra money by working as a gateman and steward on match days at the Clarence Street rugby league ground. But if robbery was the motive, why were there no signs of a break-in and why had the next-door-neighbour not been aware of any signs of commotion or struggle apart from what was described as a 'scraping noise' between 9 p.m. and 9.30 p.m. on the Saturday? Capstick dissected the facts and decided that Wyld had been killed by someone he knew, a murderer who had let himself out of the house with a front door key.

Later front-page reports chillingly detailed the manner of Walter Wyld's death. Two major stab wounds to the chest had caused massive haemorrhaging. In defending himself, the victim sustained multiple bruises, thirteen lacerations to one hand and six to the other. He died fighting frantically after returning home from a whist drive at the rugby league ground, leaving at about 9.50 p.m. on Saturday 27 January.

Over subsequent days, Capstick's men examined every inch of Walter Wyld's terrace home, later revealing the discovery of a cache of £1 and 10s bank notes in an old gas stove kept in a cupboard under the stairs and a single fingerprint found in the room where the murder took place. They also recovered a thick bundle of letters in the kitchen. Not far from Huntington Road, a constable also found a piece of stained cloth on land opposite York Fever Hospital. This was despatched for forensic examination and the hunt was on for a suspect, several interviewees collaborating in their descriptions of a suspicious pale-faced man of about 30 years of age who had been spotted near the murder scene.

In an unprecedented deployment of resources, Capstick cast his net far and wide, officers questioning over 3,000 people. An appeal for help was flashed on York cinema screens at the beginning of every performance. Broadcast loudspeaker announcements were made at the York versus Barrow rugby league game and at the soccer match between York City Reserves and Mansfield Town Reserves. Capstick also ordered his officers to visit York schools, telling all pupils to be vigilant in the search for the murder weapon. The quest for that knife was a fevered one involving hours of laborious fingertip searching. Eventually two knives were recovered by magnetic probe from the riverbed underneath Yearsley Bridge. At the same time, scores of officers followed up reports that Walter Wyld had been seen in the company of a man in military uniform.

A kind, considerate and gregarious man, Walter Wyld had been in the habit of loaning money to relatives and friends, a letter from a former neighbour found in the cache discovered in the kitchen shifting attention to the Fulford Army Camp just 4 miles from the scene of the murder. Postmarked 'Kirkcaldy, Fife' and dated 9 January 1951, the letter read:

Dear Walter,
I have just come in and got your letter. I was very pleased to hear from you until I read about the money. I hope you will remember that I paid you that money off the third pay I drew from Rowntrees. I was grateful for the loan when I got it, Walter, and I am sorry you think I left without paying. I had to come home in a hurry because my mother had an accident or else I would have been to see you. Jock is back in York now, so whenever I get his address I will tell him to come and see you.

Yours sincerely
I. Dand (Mrs)

Intrigued by the letter, Capstick made further enquiries which revealed that the Dand family had lived a few doors away from 199 Huntington Road. They formed a friendship with Walter Wyld that continued after their relocation to St Paul's Square in York and latterly to Scotland. Ex-soldier and Military Medal holder John (Jock) Dand had been invalided out of the army with duodenal ulcers. He returned to York alone on 7 January.

Dand spent much of his time in the Sergeants' Mess in the Fulford Barracks, enquiries there yielding an address. Officers visited Dand's lodgings in Burlington Avenue and brought him in for questioning on Wednesday 31 January, just four days after the murder.

Capstick conducted the interrogation, describing Dand as 'dark, lean, straight as a ramrod' and speaking 'like a typical regimental sergeant major. His eyes were hard and watchful in his long, thin face.' When he was asked when he had last seen Walter Wyld, he replied in a thick Scots burr: 'About Monday 8 January. I called at his house, had a chat in the kitchen and gave him three pounds I had borrowed from him.' When asked about his movements on the night of the murder, he replied: 'I can prove I did not kill him.' Capstick asked Dand to surrender the clothing he was wearing on 27 January and then instructed Sergeant Plater to take a written statement. In his testimony, Dand explained that he had spent the evening drinking in various York pubs with Sergeant McIrvine from the Fulford Barracks, finally leaving his friend about 10.45 p.m. and returning directly to his lodgings. The verbatim account was read back to Dand and he signed it, seeming quite unconcerned, although Capstick noted that throughout the interview he chain-smoked, with not a trace of nicotine stains on his fingers.

Taken back to his lodgings, Dand produced a blue suit, a mackintosh coat, a blue-striped shirt and a pair of brown suede shoes. Searching the premises, Sergeant Plater also removed several personal letters from a dressing-table drawer. The officer left Dand alone. He was free – for now.

Two of the confiscated letters were from Walter Wyld. The first letter read:

Dear Mr. Dand,
Just a line to let you know I am still at the above address. I called tonight at 30 St Paul's Square and they told me you had gone back to Scotland. I was surprised when I heard you had left York and not been to see me. I shall be

pleased if you will send me the money I loaned you as soon as possible. I can just do with it as my rates are due now. Hoping you are all well. Kind regards.

Yours sincerely
W. Wyld.

The second of Wyld's letters was addressed to Mrs Dand as follows:

Dear Mrs. Dand,
Your letter to hand this morning, and very pleased to hear from you. I think there is a misunderstanding somewhere. I am quite aware you paid me the £3 I lent you. About three weeks after you went to St Paul's Square, Jock came to see me and I lent him another £3 which has not been repaid, so I think that clears you. Did you not know about that? I am sorry if you did not know. Anyhow, he may come to see me and explain . . .

Yours sincerely
W. Wyld.

Both letters raised serious questions about the veracity of Dand's statement suggesting payment of the £3 debt. A third, unusually signed, letter from Mrs Dand to her husband only magnified the doubts:

Dear Jock,
There are two letters I received this week and I think you should have them. The first one was addressed to Mr. and Mrs. I still have the envelope if you don't believe me. I should have told Walter that you are in York so I expect he will be looking out for you. I hope you are very proud of yourself.

Mrs. Dand.

Capstick decided to enquire further into the background of his principal suspect, discovering a trail of debts and a level of personal expenditure not

Walter Wyld's murder monopolised the front pages. This headline is from the *York Evening Press* for 3 February 1951. (*York Evening Press*)

Knife Recovered In York Murder Hunt

ALTHOUGH Superintendent J. Capstick, of Scotland Yard, to-day officially ruled out the possibility that the knife recovered by magnet late last night from the River Foss at Yearsley Bridge, was the weapon used by the murderer to stab 72-year-old Walter Wyld at his Hunting-ton-road home matched by income. Subsequent interviews with Sergeant Irvine and Edward Hutton, another Scot temporarily domiciled in York, confirmed that Dand had been drinking with both men in the bar of the Golden Fleece in Pavement on the night of the murder. But crucially, according to their recollections, he left their company at 9.20 p.m., excusing himself with the words: 'I've got to go to keep an important date. I'm meeting a girl who is going to get me a job. I'll come back if I have time.'

By this time, forensic examination of Dand's clothing had revealed blood-staining. The blood group was A – the same type as Walter Wyld's. Dand, whose blood type was O, was brought in for further questioning.

In the presence of Inspector Wild, Capstick confronted Dand, saying: 'We've checked your movements on Saturday night last, and find you have told us a pack of lies. You said you were in the company of Sergeant McIrvine until 10.45 p.m.' Dand admitted he left the Fleece much earlier and uttered the monumental words: 'I'll tell you the truth.'

His interrogator waited in absolute silence. For ten agonising uninterrupted minutes the two men stared at each other, neither saying a word. Years later, Capstick remembered the strained and surreal atmosphere in that interview room. He recalled one of the most tense standoffs of his career in his book *Given in Evidence*, published in 1960. 'And remember – this time, a man's life was at stake!'

Eventually, Dand spoke. 'I left my pals and picked up a woman who was walking away from the Elephant and Castle,' he explained, painting a graphic picture of what happened between the pair on the river bank. Pressed on the presence of blood on his trousers, he told Capstick that it must have been menstrual blood, but despite intense questioning he refused to divulge the woman's name. 'I disbelieve your story,' answered Capstick. 'I must tell you now that it's normal blood.' With this, Dand lowered his head, shielded his eyes and muttered a phrase that barristers were later to ravage with all their courtroom guile: 'I admit that we had a row about money. It was an accident and I left him there.' At this point Capstick interjected with a formal caution and the game appeared to be up, Dand making a verbal statement in which he admitted leaving the Fleece at around 9.15 p.m. and meeting the anonymous woman. In conclusion, Capstick expected a confession. What he got was a parting shot that completely floored him. 'I now deny going to Walter Wyld's house on the Saturday night he was murdered', Dand said boldly. The contradictory claim came within minutes of the previous admission but it made no difference to Capstick's resolve. That same day, John Dand, a 32-year-old married man with two children from Kirkaldy in Scotland, was formally arrested and charged with the murder of Walter Wyld.

Dand was arraigned before York Magistrates on 5 February. After the briefest of appearances, he was remanded in custody, Capstick and his dedicated group of fellow officers compiling a detailed case against the accused, who was put before magistrates on three subsequent dates before a full trial at Leeds Crown Court.

Detective Chief Superintendent Capstick was unaware of it at the time but the four days beginning on 23 April were to be the most professionally difficult of his career. Aided in the opening hours of the trial by Crown representative Mr H.B.H. Hylton-Foster KC, MP (the barrister was soon called away on urgent parliamentary business), Capstick was confronted by Mr H.R.B. Shepherd KC and Mr G. Veale KC, two of the shrewdest veteran counsels in the legal profession. 'I was left alone to face as tough a barrage as any poor copper ever experienced,' noted Capstick in his book. 'Right from the off Mr Shepherd turned his big guns on me, challenging the way in which I was using my notebook in giving evidence.' Things turned even more serious under the defending counsels' cross-examination, Capstick, and Plater and Wild in turn being virtually accused of collusion and fabrication in suggesting that Dand had uttered the fateful phrase: 'I admit that we had a row about money. It was an accident and I left him there.' It was pointed out to the jury that the implausible and contradictory phrase interspersed between two vigorous denials had been allegedly uttered while Wild was elsewhere, Shepherd suggesting that this was a deliberate ploy by the two officers from Scotland Yard who concocted their incriminating admission when the local detective was absent from the interview room. 'Members of the jury,' said Shepherd, 'is that sufficient evidence to make you think twice before saying it is not enough? Is that evidence on which you would hang a dog? I make no bones about it. In my submission, that evidence of the admission or the alleged admission is not truthful. It is wholly inconsistent with what happened before.' The prosecutor theatrically addressed the jurors, describing Capstick as being of a frightening and intimidating mien, suggesting that most people would wilt and become confused under detailed questioning by a dominating man with such a fearsome reputation. In such circumstances, it would have been natural, he insisted, for Dand to be confused.

But the jury were having none of it. Within little more than an hour of retiring, they delivered a guilty verdict and John Dand was condemned to death by Justice Gorman on 26 April 1951. Dand was executed by hanging on 12 June in Manchester, the *York Evening Press* reporting his death in a short paragraph. In a legal world currently dominated by the procrastination of lawyers and barristers and by criminal apologists and political correctness, it is worth reflecting on the alacrity of 1950s justice. John Dand murdered Walter Wynd on 27 January. Just twenty weeks later, he too was dead.

'Though he gave me the toughest job of my career,' wrote Capstick, 'I have always felt sorry for John Dand, who committed brutal murder for a paltry debt of three pounds. I believe that, like many fine soldiers, he was a fish out of water in civilian life. Had he been able to remain in the Army, the environment which he understood and loved, his story might have had a very different and more honourable ending.'

In 1960, Capstick retired to a luxury flat on Worthing seafront, having solved more murders in provincial Britain than any other officer in the history of the Murder Squad. In thirty-two years as a policeman he had achieved almost legendary status, becoming one of the so-called 'Big Five'. 'If the police were allowed to put as much energy into chasing criminals as persecuting the motorist,' he later complained, having taken to enjoying the open road in a brand new Citroën car, 'there would not be the big increase in successful crime that we are now seeing.'

18

INTO THE VALLEY OF DEATH

VC: two simple letters convey as much heroism and pathos as those 55 lines of the famously shivering poem by Alfred Lord Tennyson. The Victoria Cross – our nation's ultimate gallantry award for valour – was partly designed by Queen Victoria herself in 1856 to acknowledge the debt owed to British and Commonwealth heroes in battle. Applied retrospectively to the Crimean conflict that began in 1854, the honour has since been awarded 1,354 times. A 23-year-old York man was one of its first recipients.

Thomas Wilkinson was originally a resident of Marygate. Born on 4 December 1831, the son of an agricultural labourer and a dressmaker, he joined the army voluntarily in York in 1850 and served as a gunner in the Royal Marine Artillery on board HMS *Britannia* at Sebastopol. During her voyage, the ship was afflicted with cholera as she negotiated the Dardanelles. Many soldiers died of the disease, but Wilkinson survived and saw action, using the ship's cannon on the heights overlooking Balaklava on 25 October 1854. He was in the thick of the fighting again on 5 November at Inkerman, but it was on the hills above the highly strategic port of Sebastopol, which had resisted blockade, siege and sustained bombardments throughout the winter months, that Wilkinson found himself next.

The British and French artillery opened up on the Redan – the port's principal fortification – on 6 June 1855. Wilkinson was stationed in the advanced batteries opposing the Russian guns when, during the third of six bombardments on 7 June, heavy fire threatened to destroy his position. Salvo after salvo degraded the embrasures and parapets surrounding the British guns, leaving men and ordnance vulnerable to rifle fire and exploding shells and shrapnel. Oblivious to the danger, Wilkinson courageously repaired the damage, tossing sandbags into the breaches, one contemporary newspaper recording his gallantry with the words: 'while bullets were flying around and shot and shell falling thick, he sprang to the top of the earth work and calling on his comrades to bring sandbags, began the repair of the parapet, until, by his exertions, cover was restored'. His considerable bravery was noted by his commanding officer, his glowing testimony of Wilkinson's courage being reflected in a letter from Colonel Wesley, Deputy Adjutant General Royal Marines sent to the *London Gazette* and published on

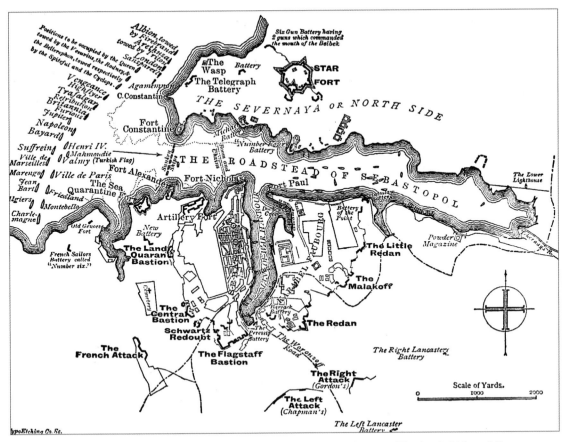

Plan of Sebastopol showing the defence. *(From* Cassell's History of England, *Volume VI, in VIII volumes ending in 1898)*

24 February 1857: 'Specially recommended for gallant conduct in the advance Batteries, 7th June 1855, in placing sandbags to repair the work under a galling fire; his name having been sent up on the occasions, as worthy of special notice, by the Commanding Officer of the Artillery of the Right Attack.'

Wilkinson's obvious bravery had an immediate impact on his career. He was promoted to Bombardier in December 1855 and ordered to join the company of HMS *Mohawk* the following February. By April 1856, he was assigned to yet another ship, but he missed her embarkation and his service was blighted with a court martial. Interestingly, the official records kept in the Royal Marines Museum in Southsea do not state the charge, and although he was found guilty and temporarily demoted back to the rank of Gunner, his name was never entered into the so-called Divisional Defaulters' Book. Were the records tampered with? By this time, Wilkinson must have been nominated for a VC and it would hardly have been consistent for the honour to be conferred on a man who had been publicly disgraced with a court martial. In any event, the hero was

reinstated as a Bombardier and, shortly afterwards, he became the fourteenth recipient of the VC.

Wilkinson received his award from Queen Victoria at the first investiture at Hyde Park on 26 June 1857, sixty-one other winners also receiving their medals that day. Over 100,000 ordinary spectators were assembled in the park together with 12,000 VIPs, accommodated in a vast semi-circle of seats. The Queen, who was accompanied by the Prince Consort, Prince Frederick William of Prussia, and a 'brilliant military suite', elected to stay on horseback during the presentations, her awkwardness in performing the pinning on of the medals spawning an abiding legend. Her Majesty 'was leaning forward from the saddle like a Cossack with a lance', relates a contemporary account, 'when she stabbed one of the recipients with the medal pin'. In true heroic fashion, the man received the medal into his flesh without flinching. Wilkinson was unscathed as a march-past by 4,000 soldiers brought the glittering occasion to a close. The historic investiture, described in the Prince Consort's diary as 'a superb spectacle', was later captured on canvas by the talented artist George H. Thomas. In acknowledgement of his considerable bravery, Wilkinson also received the French Legion of Honour and the Turkish and British Crimea Medals, the latter with clasps for service at Balaklava, Inkerman and Sebastopol.

Wilkinson went on to serve aboard HMS *Mersey* in March 1859; he was discharged, having served nearly nine years of his twelve-year enlistment, in October on the grounds of 'lameness contracted in not by the service'.

After his retirement from the Royal Marine Artillery and a spell as a Sergeant Instructor for Auxiliary Forces, he returned to his native York. Ironically, he secured a job as the manager of Rymer's Sand Yard in North Street where he lived. He died of exhaustion and diarrhoea at the age of 55 on 22 September 1887 and was buried in a public grave – one of ten bodies – in York Cemetery. His interment was accompanied by full military honours, twenty-four men of the Leicester Regiment providing his honour guard. A headstone was later erected by the officers, NCOs and men of his regiment as a token of their esteem and respect.

Although Victoria Crosses are traditionally manufactured from the intrinsically almost worthless metal taken from guns captured during the Crimean War (it seems that some Chinese ordnance has inadvertently been used from time to time), as historical and collectors' items they are invaluable and command high prices. It is fortunate, then, that Wilkinson's medal, which was put up for sale in 1918, did not fall into the hands of a private collector but was bought by officers of the Royal Marines Artillery at Eastney. Today, it is one of the principal attractions at their museum in Southsea.

Thomas Wilkinson is in the van of a contingent of York heroes who fought in the Crimea, William Bentley of the 11th Hussars, William Pearson of the 17th Lancers and Private John Hogan bringing glory to the white rose. All three

Opposite: Sketch of the assault on the Redan. *(From* Cassell's History of England, *Volume VI)*

comrades fought with gallantry during the historic but futile and utterly disastrous Charge of the Light Brigade at Balaklava on 25 October 1854: 'Into the valley of Death/Rode the six hundred'.

One of the most curiously celebrated blunders in military history that stirred a nation and whose 'fame has rung through all lands and still permeates every army', the charge was the consequence of poor intelligence about the disposition of artillery, garbled and confused orders and professional rivalry between Lord Lucan and Lord Cardigan. The suicide mission by the brigade of 673 mounted men into a valley heavily defended by cannon, multiple small arms and a detachment of cavalry resulted in 157 dead and over 100 wounded or missing. Some 325 horses were mown down and only 195 mounted men were left after the carnage – but 'Theirs not to reason why,/Theirs but to do and die' in an attack that lasted just twenty minutes.

During the gallop, Private William Pearson, who enlisted in Dublin in 1848 and served under the command of fellow Yorkshireman Sir George Orby Wombwell of Newburgh Priory near Coxwold, received a lance wound in his side. Riding nearby, Sergeant William Bentley was attacked from behind by three Cossacks and wounded in the neck. In mortal peril, he was rescued by Lieutenant A.R. Dunn, who killed the assailants, thereby earning a Victoria Cross. Pearson was hospitalised after the disaster and was sent to Scutari, where he was personally nursed by the legendary Florence Nightingale.

Pearson recovered from his wounds and, although he was certified only for non-combatant duties as a depot orderly, he volunteered to accompany his regiment in its deployment to India, where he served with distinction throughout the Mutiny. He was discharged from the army in 1861 to become a turnkey at York Castle. After retirement from prison duties, he lived with relatives in Walmgate, sustained by a sizeable pension of 1s a day, awarded to all survivors of the Charge of the Light Brigade from an appeal fund set up in 1894 at the instigation of the editor of *Illustrated Bits*, T.H. Roberts.

Bentley became a drill instructor with the Royal Wiltshire Regiment, eventually retiring to York in 1884 after completing thirty-seven years' military service. He died in 1891 and was buried with full military honours in York Cemetery. At the graveside were his old comrades Pearson and Hogan. They were buried in nearby plots. Pearson, the last of the illustrious trio, died in 1909. Rifle volleys were fired over his grave by men of the 5th Royal Irish Lancers.

The Crimean War was, for the most part, a disastrous episode in European military history, almost as many men falling foul of rampant disease as enemy action. Amazed at the unsanitary conditions, one Yorkshire volunteer wrote the following words home to his despairing mother: 'When we came here first we were put in the largest barracks in the world. They are able to hold thousands upon thousands but there is no convenience. There are no beds or bedding of any kind. We huddled together like as many pigs. We should have soon all been filthy but they removed us to camp.' Another newly arrived recruit, Florence Nightingale, was also appalled at the conditions, writing: 'the wind blew sewer air up the pipes of numerous open privies into the rooms. As the privies were choked, large wooden tubs stood there to receive ordure.'